FROM PACHOMIUS TO IGNATIUS

FROM PACHOMIUS TO IGNATIUS

A STUDY IN THE CONSTITUTIONAL HISTORY OF THE RELIGIOUS ORDERS

by
DAVID KNOWLES

THE SARUM LECTURES
1964–5

CLARENDON PRESS
OXFORD
1966

Oxford University Press, Ely House, London W.1

GLASGOW NEW YORK TORONTO MELBOURNE WELLINGTON
CAPE TOWN SALISBURY IBADAN NAIROBI LUSAKA ADDIS ABABA
BOMBAY CALCUTTA MADRAS KARACHI LAHORE DACCA
KUALA LUMPUR HONG KONG

Printed in Great Britain by
Butler & Tanner Ltd, Frome and London

CONTENTS

FOREWORD

THIS book contains in substance the Sarum Lectures delivered before the University of Oxford in Michaelmas Term, 1964. My gratitude is due to the Electors to the Sarum Lectureship for inviting me to deliver them and to the Delegates of the Clarendon Press for accepting them for publication under their imprint. The repeated visits to Oxford were, as always, made memorable by contacts with both senior and junior members of the university expert in medieval and monastic history, and by the hospitality of friends.

The form of the lectures did not seem to demand elaborate bibliographical notes. For those who wish to read further in the evolution of the monastic way of life historical and general information on all monastic and religious orders can be found in M. Heimbucher, *Die Orden und Kongregationen der katholischen Kirche* (3rd ed., Paderborn, 1933–4). For traditional Benedictine monachism the best general historical account is that of Ph. Schmitz, *Histoire de l'Ordre de saint Benoît* (7 vols., Maredsous, 1943–56); the best, indeed the only, critical and analytical study is that of E. C. Butler, *Benedictine Monachism* (2nd. ed., London, 1924, reprinted Cambridge, 1961). Good discussions, with bibliographies, of all monastic topics are often to be found in one of the great French dictionaries: *Dictionnaire de théologie catholique* (complete; Paris, 1905–50), *Dictionnaire d'archéologie chrétienne et de liturgie* (complete; Paris, 1907–53), *Dictionnaire d'histoire et de géographie ecclésiastiques* (in progress, Paris 1912–), *Dictionnaire de spiritualité* (in progress, Paris, 1932–). The most useful survey of the whole field of monastic studies is Dom P. Cousin's *Précis d'histoire monastique* (Paris, 1956), but the reader must be on the watch for small errors, faults of nomenclature, and misprints.

David Knowles

I

FROM PACHOMIUS TO BENEDICT OF ANIANE

THE history of the monastic order in the West during the Middle Ages, and the history of the religious orders that sprang from its parent stem, may be considered in a variety of aspects. We may consider them as a purely religious force, with their spiritual teaching, their examples of holiness, and their lessons of decline. We may consider them as a social and economic phenomenon, as a part of medieval society, as producers, farmers, capitalists, and consumers, or as a bulwark of the clerical as opposed to the lay institutions of their times. We may consider them also as a great cultural force, as the greatest single agency in transmitting the legacy of the past, as an important factor in the higher education of the renaissance of the twelfth century, as patrons of architecture and sculpture, as the only artists in calligraphy and illumination during the greater part of the Middle Ages.

All these are historically important aspects of the religious orders, but the present study will concentrate attention upon a less familiar topic, the development, that is, stage by stage, of the fully articulated and integrated religious order in the western Church. This development, though it has received far less attention than the development of feudal or parliamentary institutions, may well be considered one of the most remarkable achievements of the medieval genius, comparable to the development of scholastic thought or of the plan and design of a great cathedral. Important and intellectually fascinating in itself, this achievement has had an influence on all succeeding ages. Not only have the greater medieval orders continued in existence to the present day in almost exactly the same form, but later orders, such as the Jesuits in the sixteenth century, adopted their main features while adapting them to the needs of another world, and the many modern orders of men and women, missionaries, teachers, and nurses, whatever their specific differences, have as their generic basis the leading principles laid down in the twelfth and thirteenth centuries. In addition, many of their characteristic features were copied or reproduced in a number of civic constitutions of the Middle Ages, and their ghost or skeleton is with us in our orders of chivalry. Yet it is only in the present century that some individual constitutions have been studied, and so far as I am aware the long process of evolution has never been reviewed.

The great constitutional development took place within a little more than two hundred years, from the abbacy of Odilo at Cluny, which began in 994, to the death of St. Dominic in 1221, but we must needs overlap this period at both ends: in earlier centuries, to see what previous intimations or experiments there may have been; and in later centuries, and especially in the origins of the Jesuit order, to see what improvements or corrections the new circumstances of the modern world may have called forth.

As we shall see, our study must begin with the Rule of St. Benedict, composed about 535. From that short document, quite literally, as from a seed, the whole organization grew. But although the Rule, for western Europe at least, was institutionally speaking the acorn, the monastic life, and in some instances a highly organized form of that life, had a history of two and a half centuries behind it when St. Benedict wrote. It had originated in Egypt shortly before the reign of Constantine. It was, in the words of an eminent Byzantinist of yesterday, Norman Baynes, 'Egypt's greatest gift to the world'; and he added, 'what monasticism has meant in the history of Europe cannot easily be calculated.'[1] Monasticism, as its etymology (*μόνος*—alone) suggests, began with an individual's retirement from the world. St. Anthony the

[1] N. H. Baynes and H. St. L. B. Moss, *Byzantium* (Oxford, 1948), introd. by N. H. Baynes, xxxi.

Great (251–356), usually known as the first monk, was in fact an anchorite and not the first of that family, but unlike the 'pure' hermits, such as St. Paul of Egypt, he ultimately became the leader of a numerous family, to whom he gave instructions and permanent help even when he had retired finally into the desert land near the Red Sea.[1] But in our story the first name is Pachomius (286–346), the father of monks of the common life, who, like St. Benedict, began as an anchorite but became in 315, as he thought under divine inspiration, the founder of a family of monks living and working together. Recruits came in floods, and when he died he was the father of a large group of monasteries containing possibly 5,000 inmates.[2] Besides writing a Rule, Pachomius also organized every detail of a great institution, and this it is that gives him his significance for our purpose. When he died, we might almost say that a perfect monastic order was in existence. Not only was all the material framework there—church, refectory, assembly room, cells, enclosure wall—not only was the daily life of prayer and work in all its parts arranged, not only was the spiritual discipline of chastity, poverty, and obedience wisely established, but the whole complex was knit together by firm strands of control.[3]

[1] For St. Anthony see L. Bouyer, *Vie de saint Antoine* (Saint-Wandrille, 1950) and *Studia Anselmiana* 38, 'Antonius Magnus eremita. Studia ad antiquum monachismum spectantia', ed. B. Steidle (Rome, 1956). The *Vita Antonii*, written in Greek by St. Athanasius, must still be read in the edition of B. de Montfaucon, reprinted by Migne, *Patrologia Graeca* XXVI. 837–976. There is an English translation by R. Mayer, *The Life of St. Anthony* newly translated and annotated (Westminster, Maryland, 1950). See also K. Heussi, *Der Ursprung des Mönchtums* (Tübingen, 1936).

[2] The Rule of Pachomius in its long version exists only in the Latin translation of St. Jerome, of which a critical edition by A. Boon was published with other documents by T. Lefort (Louvain, 1932). See also the articles 'Cénobitisme' and 'Pakhôme' in *Dict. Arch. Chrét. Lit.* by H. Leclercq, ii. 2. 3118 ff. and xiii. 499 ff. The work of P. Ladeuze, *Étude sur le cénobitisme pakhomien pendant le iv*e *siècle et la première moitié du v*e (Louvain, 1898) is still valuable.

[3] H. Bacht, 'L'importance de l'idéal monastique chez saint Pachôme pour l'histoire du monachisme chrétien', in *Revue d'ascétique et de*

Within each monastery were numerous houses, each containing thirty or forty monks practising a particular craft. These houses might be themselves thirty or forty in number, making up a settlement of 1,500 or 2,000 souls. Within the houses were parties of ten or so under a foreman. Each house was governed by a master, and each monastery by a father or abbot. Pachomius himself remained at the head and lived in the head house of the whole institute. At every level the superior could direct and transfer his monks, and at every level there were regular reunions for spiritual conference and advice. In the monasteries there was, alongside the abbot, a minister who dealt with all economic matters— supplies of food and raw materials, distribution and sale of necessaries and products. Pachomius visited all the houses repeatedly, and twice a year there was a general gathering in his monastery. At Easter all came up to celebrate the Pasch and to baptize any catechumens, and at mid-August all the procurators or ministers came up to render an account of the year's working. It was a remarkable achievement of planning and discipline.

The golden age of the Pachomian system probably ended with its founder. In any case, we need not pursue its history, for it had no great influence on other regions in its epoch, and if, as has been suggested, it affected the shape of European monachism centuries later, it was through its literary monuments alone. Meanwhile, monasticism spread to Syria and Palestine, and later to Asia Minor with Basil of Caesarea, St. Basil the Great (330–79). St. Basil is the father and patriarch of Orthodox monachism more truly, even, than St. Benedict is of western monastic life, but he need not detain us now.[1] Though he wrote no Rule, his conferences and replies to questions were treated as a guide and were quoted as a rule by St. Benedict and others. He formed no congregation or order, but he made of his monasteries homes of charity,

mystique (1950), 308–26, and 'Antonius und Pachomius' in *Studia Anselmiana* 38 (1956), 66–107.

[1] W. R. Lowther Clarke, *St. Basil the Great* (Cambridge, 1913), and *The Ascetic Works of St. Basil* (London, 1925).

containing orphanages, hospitals, workhouses, farms, and hospices, in this respect anticipating the western orders of the later Middle Ages.

The spread of monasticism to the West is one of the most striking phenomena of the patristic age. It did not pass as an organism but as a germ; that is to say, it was not conveyed to western Europe in its organized form by a group under a leader, as western institutes have been conveyed in modern times to the East, but it was carried by hearsay, by individuals, and above all by the exiled Athanasius and his *Life of St. Anthony*, one of the formative books of Christian spirituality. Yet its penetration was at first slow, almost furtive.

Though the first traces can be found in the West before 350, a famous passage of St. Augustine's *Confessions*[1] tells us that he was unaware of its existence in the West and even in Milan, where he had been living for several years, as late as 386. The germ of monasticism, whether we regard it under the metaphor of a disease or of a plant, took different forms in reaction to host, soil, and climate, appearing in Africa and Italy in the community of the bishop's household of clerks, in Italy again and elsewhere in an army of hermits, and in Gaul in the quasi eremitical settlement of St. Martin.[2] From Gaul it passed to Ireland, Wales and the Western Isles in a novel and socially very remarkable Celtic and tribal form. In none of these manifestations, however, was there any overhead organization. Even in Ireland in the great age of monasticism, 550–650, the only association between monasteries was what may be called the natural one of mother house to daughter house, which, as in the case of individuals, ceased when the younger attained maturity. The confederation of mutual intercession, with set prayers for the dead of each house, was again natural and common, but of no constitutional interest.[3]

[1] *Confessions*, ed. J. Gibb and W. Montgomery (2 ed., Cambridge, 1927), VIII. cc. 14–15, pp. 216–18.

[2] *Studia Anselmiana* 46, 'Saint Martin et son temps; Mémorial du xvie centénaire des débuts du monachisme en Gaule' (Rome, 1961).

[3] J. Ryan, *Irish Monasticism* (Dublin, 1931).

The first fixed point in the constitutional history of western monachism is the *Rule of St. Benedict of Nursia*, written *c.* 535–45. It is true that the originality of that Rule is under heavy attack in our day, that in it there is no mention of the slightest connection with any other house, and that in fact it was more than a century before it was widely used. Nevertheless, whatever may be the indebtedness of St. Benedict to the *Regula Magistri*, it was he who first set out with lapidary brevity the outline of domestic government, and when at last a wide organization was constructed, the monastery governed by the Rule was at its base, and in time many of the enactments of the Rule became decrees of canon law.[1]

The key points of the Rule were: the monarchical abbot, elected for life by his monks, and himself appointing his officials;[2] the general gathering of all the brethren to council on all matters of grave common interest, and the smaller council of seniors to advise the abbot on matters of lesser importance;[3] and the vow of stability binding the monk to life-long residence in the monastery of his profession.[4] The Rule thus deals only with a single self-contained, self-supporting, and self-sufficient family. There is no suggestion of any supervision by an external authority, save that of the bishop in the case of a notoriously culpable abbot,[5] no hint of any association for discipline or legislation, no instructions even to govern the making of new foundations, though St. Benedict made at least one, at Terracina.

The traditional picture of Benedictine monachism spreading over the map of Europe like oil from Monte Cassino has

[1] The best critical edition is that of R. Hanslik, *Benedicti Regula* in *Corpus Scriptorum Ecclesiasticorum Latinorum* LXXV (Vienna, 1960). The *editio critico-practica* of E. C. Butler (3 ed., Freiburg-im-Breisgau, 1935) is still valuable for the indication of sources and presentation of the doctrine of St. Benedict. For English readers the annotated translation by J. McCann is recommended (London, 1952). References to the Rule are by chapter and 'verse' as first printed by A. Lentini in his edition (1947) and followed by Hanslik.

[2] LXIV. 1–3; cf. XXI. 3, LXV. 11, LXXI. 3.

[3] III. [4] LVIII. 15, IV. 78. [5] LXIV. 4; cf. LXII. 9.

been obliterated by modern research. It is improbable that the community survived as a group the sack of the abbey by the Lombards in 581;[1] improbable, also, that St. Gregory the Great or his disciple St. Augustine of Canterbury followed the Rule as a code.[2] As late as 950 there is no certainty that any of the Roman monasteries were 'Benedictine'.[3] There is, however, certainty that observance of the Rule spread gradually in France and England, and that by the time of Charlemagne it was the common code of most of the monasteries of his Empire, though extended and in some cases obscured by liturgical and other customs and 'uses'.

Charlemagne was not a great patron or founder of monasteries, but he had in their regard the same love of uniformity, wide vision as a legislator, and sense of the value of the basic classical document that he showed in so many fields. His question. 'Is there any Rule other than that of Benedict?' shows how matters stood at least in northern France, and his mission to Monte Cassino for a copy reputed to be the autograph of the patriarch is characteristic.[4] Towards the end of his reign he decreed that all monks should observe the Rule, but he died before he had taken any decisive steps to effect this.

[1] S. Brechter, 'Monte Cassino's erste Zerstörung', in *Studien u. Mitteilungen z. Geschichte des Benediktinerordens* LVI (1938), 109–50.

[2] K. Hallinger, 'Papst Gregor der Grosse und der Hl. Benedikt', in *Studia Anselmiana* 42 (1957), 231–320.

[3] G. Ferrari, *Early Roman Monasteries* (Vatican City, 1957), p. 220: 'There is no evidence of a monastery in Rome which employed exclusively the Rule of St. Benedict much before the tenth century.' On which B. F. Hamilton, in an unpublished Ph.D. thesis of London University (1960), 'The Holy See, the Roman nobility and the Ottonian emperors', p. 233, comments: 'It is difficult to justify the qualification "much", because there is no evidence in any of the sources that the Rule of S. Benedict was used exclusively in any Roman monastery until after the first visit of S. Odo in 936.'

[4] The (probably authentic) covering letter sent by Abbot Theodomar to Charlemagne has often been printed, e.g. by E. Dümmler, *Mon. Germ. Hist. Epistolae* 4 (1895), 509–14, and B. Albers, *Constitutiones Monasticae* III. (1907), 50–65; also, with full apparatus, in *Corpus Consuetudinum Monasticarum*, ed. K. Hallinger, I (1964), 157–75.

His son Louis the Pious carried on his father's designs. He had used for many years a reforming abbot of Languedoc, Benedict of Aniane, to establish discipline and uniformity in Aquitaine; now, he summoned him to court, and built for him the abbey of Inden (815) near Aachen, to serve as a model and nursery for the Empire. Beyond this, in order to secure the uniformity desired by his father, he summoned the abbots of the Empire to gatherings at Aachen in August 816, in July 817, and July 818. Abbot Benedict conducted proceedings and the decisions on observance were registered in the official records of the meetings.[1] He also presented the monks with two long compilations, a *Codex regularum*,[2] or collection of eastern and western Rules, and the *Concordia regularum*,[3] a commentary on the Rule of St. Benedict consisting largely of extracts from other Rules designed to show the excellence of St. Benedict's selection and the superiority of the article finished by him. Uniformity was the keynote of the whole exercise, and it is possible that we may possess a striking memorial of this ideal. The celebrated plan of a monastic complex, including provision for almost all the services of a welfare state and known as the plan of St. Gall, may well be a copy or 'blue-print' of the plan circulated by Abbot Benedict for the instruction of those about to design or reconstruct a large abbey.[4]

The scheme of Louis the Pious, like many other Carolingian projects, was too magnificent for the age. Salutary capitularies might abound, but there was no administrative machinery to keep the great body going. Abbot Benedict, the only visible leader, died prematurely four years after the great assembly, the Emperor Louis ran into trouble, and the Caro-

[1] The whole corpus of decrees, &c., is printed with full critical apparatus in *Corp. Const. Mon.* I. 423–81, 503–36. There are excellent bibliographical notes.

[2] Migne, *P.L.* CIII. 393–664, reprinting L. Holstein (Rome, 1661), ii. 293–462.

[3] Migne, ibid. 703–1380, reprinting H. Ménard (Paris, 1638).

[4] H. Reinhardt, *Die Karolingische Klosterplan von St. Gallen* (St. Gall, 1952).

lingian Empire broke up and foundered. Nevertheless, the work accomplished was not wholly a waste of energy. It remained a memory and a norm, with documentary monuments, to which all similar reforms adjusted themselves in the centuries that immediately followed. Thus the procedure and aims of the English reformers, Dunstan and Ethelwold, who summoned the abbots of England to meet under the presidency of King Edgar, were a clear imitation of the meeting at Aachen, and the *Regularis Concordia* recalled the capitular decrees of Aachen. Moreover, the Carolingian project of uniting all the monasteries of Europe with the Rule as a common code gave the monasticism of the Empire for the first time the conception that all monks were a single family looking for direction and protection to a single patriarch and patron. The *monasticus ordo*, a phrase in which *ordo* signifies 'an ordered way of life', was becoming the 'household of St. Benedict', *familia S. Benedicti*, and would soon be the 'ordo S. Benedicti', but it was still a long way from being a *religiosus ordo*.

II

CLUNY, 909–1156

WE are not concerned with the general decadence, especially in France, of the monasteries, many of which were secularized in whole or in part in the late ninth century. The beginning of a new constitutional era dates from the foundation in 909, by William Count of Aquitaine, of the small monastery of Cluny in a shallow valley of the fertile country south-west of Dijon. The single peculiarity of Cluny at its foundation, which was the *sine-qua-non* of its future greatness, was its commendation to the Holy See without any intermediary. This removed it, as its founder intended, entirely out of the control both of the secular lord of the land and of the bishop, either of whom, in the conditions then obtaining, might well have appropriated it. Actually, under tenth-century conditions, when the papacy was passing through the most degrading and impotent phase of its long history, attachment to the Church of St. Peter was little more than attachment to a wraith or a vacuum, but it had the great negative virtue of separating the new foundation from all else, and leaving it free to grow if it could, and when the reformed papacy began once more to exploit its resources, Cluny was among them.

It was, however, almost a century before Cluny showed herself as a new species. Her first abbot, Berno, was no revolutionary, and her second, third, and fourth, Odo, Aymard, and Maieul, though saintly and of noble birth, were not original. Their influence was considerable, because they established the reputation of Cluny as a fervent and exemplary house, and like earlier and contemporary abbots of good fame, they were called in by nobles, bishops, and monks to guide and reform other houses; this they did, in the traditional way, by introducing the customs and atmosphere of

Cluny. Gradually, therefore, Cluny became the spiritual mother of a large family. There was, however, as yet no question of overall jursidiction or general dependence. The change came with the fourth abbot, Odilo, who came to office young in 994 and was in power for fifty-five years. At the death of Maieul only five houses depended upon Cluny; Odilo, like his predecessors, was soon charged with the reform of other houses and, unlike his predecessors, he tended of set policy to make these monasteries directly dependent upon Cluny, and thus the order of Cluny began to consolidate. Established in its main lines by Odilo (994–1049), it developed and achieved its greatest extension under his successor, Hugh the Great, a man of noble Burgundian family who, like Odilo, became abbot in his twenties and ruled Cluny for sixty years, 1049–1109.[1]

The number of dependent houses, sixty or so in 1049, rose rapidly during Hugh's reign. Their number is said to have attained two thousand, but a total is in any case difficult to arrive at, for no contemporary catalogue exists and there is no certain basis of computation when various degrees of influence enter in. It is, however, fairly easy to reckon up a thousand genuine examples of dependence in houses great and small.

The key principle of the system, which governed the whole body, was that the abbot of Cluny was the immediate superior of all the monks of the order. To him all the novices made profession, and by him all superiors were appointed. Odilo, in fact, and Hugh after him, became to the family of Cluny in

[1] There is no adequate full-scale history of Cluny. That by G. de Valous, *Le monachisme clunisien des origines au xve siècle*, 2 vols. (Paris, 1935), though useful and informative, has limitations of scope and treatment, and in particular does not attempt to analyse the organization and designs of the order and the great abbots. G. de Valous's art. in the *Dict. hist. géogr. ecclés.* and that of K. Hallinger in *Enciclopedia Italiana* are both valuable. N. Hunt (Sister M. Dolores) has dealt with the constitutional aspects of Abbot Hugh's reign in an unpublished London Ph.D. thesis (1958). There is no complete critical list of Cluniac dependencies.

the eleventh century what the popes of the thirteenth century claimed to be of all the faithful, the direct and immediate ordinary. Yet novel as was the organization of Cluniac houses as a great body of monasteries following the same way of life under the disciplinary direction of a single head, it should be clearly understood that Cluny and her dependencies did not form a religious order in the sense of the word that became standardized in the late medieval period and that has persisted to the present day. This latter sense implies a body made up either of houses or of individual religious of equal status governed by superiors or legislative bodies elected or appointed by a system giving equal power or eligibility for office to all, or at least very many, of the component members. Considered in the concrete, it is an organization made up of houses grouped into provinces, governed by a provincial and his council, and under the supreme direction of a general and his advisory or legislative assessors. It is a fully international body directed from the centre. The Cluniac system was far more primitive. It was a conflation of two ideas: the community of the Rule under an abbot, and the dominion and control of a king over his tenants-in-chief and sub-vassals. In theory every monk of every house was a member of the community of Cluny; everyone therefore was a subject of the abbot of Cluny. All professions were made to him, and any monk visiting Cluny was a member of its chapter. On the other hand, a majority of the houses of the Cluniac body were integrated by a charter specifying their obligations of obedience, limitations of autonomy, and a small annual *census* or tax. Externally therefore the relationship was one of vertical dependence, not of horizontal equality, and the model was not a commune or a federation, but the feudal bond which was being elaborately developed in contemporary Europe, and particularly in France. Cluny thus made use of the two most powerful ideas in early medieval society, that of the religious obedience of a monk to his abbot, and that of the fidelity and mutual obligations of vassal and lord. The pivot of the whole system was the abbot of Cluny, who was at once in his spiritual capacity the father and sovereign of all Cluniac monks and in his forensic capacity, as *persona* or lord of the church of Cluny, the overlord to whom all the churches linked to her owed fealty. Cluny had stumbled into empire and there was no element of reason or statecraft in her system. Each of the two elements, the relationship of monk to abbot and of vassal to lord, was in a sense artificial and false, for obedience to a titular abbot whom one never saw was an unreality, and so was the fictional feudal relationship of one monastery to another, or rather of a part of one great family to another more honourable part. Nevertheless, it worked for a time because it exactly met the capacities and estimates of value of its age.

Since the Cluniac system had not been planned but had resulted from numerous *ad hoc* decisions, it is impossible to set out a logical scheme of its members. Several groups can be distinguished, but different methods of definition would produce different and equally plausible results. Generally speaking, the norm established by Odilo was that any monastery by whom or on behalf of whom the abbot of Cluny was called in as reformer should be reduced to the rank of a priory; that its prior should be appointed by the abbot of Cluny, and that its novices should make profession to the abbot of Cluny, visiting Cluny, or at least approaching the abbot of Cluny, for that purpose. There were, however, three classes of exceptions to this rule:

A. A number of abbeys had joined the family before this practice had been established, and of these a few of the most celebrated were allowed to retain abbatial status and autonomy, though observing all Cluniac uses, and receiving an abbot nominated by the abbot of Cluny;

B. A few houses coming in later were allowed similar freedom,

C. A few abbeys were allowed to elect their own superior, subject to confirmation.

Of the houses strictly dependent on Cluny two classes can be made: (i) Cluny herself had a number of dependent priories and cells, her own offspring, like that of any other great abbey such as St. Albans. (ii) The order, strictly so-called, of houses reformed or absorbed by Cluny. All these, however powerful, save for the exceptions already referred to, were reduced to the rank of priory and were controlled by Cluny with varying degrees of influence, depending partly on their charter of aggregation and partly on their situation. The daughters of these houses fell into the net of Cluny along with the mother house. Thus the line of dependence ran from last to first: Mendham (Norfolk) dependended on Castle Acre, Castle Acre on Lewes, Lewes on Cluny. But there were innumerable small differences, and many small houses were in fact governed by the provisions of their charter of foundation as well as by their charter of affiliation. It was only in the late twelfth and thirteenth centuries, when Cluny's significance was diminished, that an order was formed with constitutional elements taken from the Cistercians.

Finally, there were near the periphery of the Cluniac circle other groups:

(*a*) Loosely attached were a number of abbeys who had adopted the Cluniac discipline and ceremonial in full, but without losing their autonomy—English examples were the royal foundations of Reading (Henry I) and Faversham (Stephen).

(*b*) On the very fringe were abbeys that had elected, or had been given, a Cluniac as abbot. He would naturally introduce certain features of Cluniac life, but not subjection to Cluny. Thus William of Dijon assisted in the foundation of Norman abbeys and became abbot of Fécamp, and Gilbert Foliot was appointed to Gloucester after holding office at Cluny and Abbeville. Indeed the Cluniac network was so extensive and her influence so pervasive that contemporaries such as Gerald of Wales and historians following their lead may be excused for their occasional use of 'Cluniac' as synonymous with 'black monk' or 'Benedictine'. There is a real distinction, however, between dependence and susceptibility to influence.

In spite of the vast extension of Cluny's family, no constitutional framework was set up. No general chapter was thought of, no devolution or delegation of powers took place. The bond was still to the abbot of Cluny alone, backed by the influence and jealous vigilance of the huge community of Cluny, recruited largely from the cream of the candidates of Europe, and housed in the most magnificent establishment of the age, Cluny, indeed, came to be, for a short time in the mid-eleventh century, the spiritual capital of Europe. That the vast organization held together, that the engine did not stall on the first grade, was due partly to the great weight attached by contemporary society to the personal relationship of lord and vassal, partly to the respect felt for a firm centre of spiritual excellence during the disastrous eclipse of the papacy, but still more to the outstanding personalities and long lives of abbots Odilo and Hugh, who between them covered 115 years. If we omit the thirteen years of the enigmatic Pons and the few days of his aged successor (1109–22) and count in the forty-six years of Maieul and the thirty-five of Peter the Venerable (1122–57) we can say that Cluny was ruled for almost exactly two centuries by four men of outstanding ability, wisdom, and piety. It is a record to which it would be hard to find a rival in any series of rulers, clerical or lay, in European history. The value of their personal qualities was increased in the second century of the period by the personal friendship between the abbots and a distinguished series of reforming popes, most of whom were monks, with more than one Cluniac among them. To depend upon, to be protected and counselled by such men, was worth much in the troubled eleventh century. If direct Cluniac influence on the Gregorian reform has been exaggerated in the past, we must not forget this background of spiritual strength in the age of the struggle between Empire and papacy.

III

THE NEW ORDERS

THUS far we have been considering a single monastic body, that of the black monks following the Rule of St. Benedict interpreted in a traditional manner. We have now to meet new ventures which, while for the most part retaining the Rule as the nucleus of their institute, devised a way of life which departed from tradition.

The great religious revival of the eleventh century is perhaps the most widespread and the most spiritual of all the mysterious religious revivals of the West. Compared with earlier renovations it had two distinctive features. In common with all medieval movements it claimed to be a return to past excellence, but whereas previously the golden age had been situated in the sixth century, reformers were now seeking their models in earlier ages, and monastic reformers were demanding a return to the desert cradle of monachism. The reform of the eleventh century was distinguished also by the spirit of the age: the new capacity of adolescent Europe to rationalize problems and organize on a wide scale was brought to bear upon the needs of the religious life, and a constitutional framework was gradually evolved that was capable of application to all kinds of vocation. In the event, reformers split the single traditional version of the monastic life into twenty different divisions, as it were the colours of the spectrum, each realizing a potentiality implicit in the monastic life but neglected by most contemporary manifestations, and thus meeting a need in the more complex and articulated society of the later Middle Ages. It was here that the history of western monachism separated from that of the Orthodox Church, where the single ray of light was never fully broken down into its component colours.

The institutes now formed in Europe were of varying importance, but several of them survived to become more fully organized and to continue to exist throughout and beyond the Middle Ages.

In general it may be said that two fields appear, divided by the western Alps. In Italy the impulse began about 1000 and was exhausted for the time by 1100. The current here set towards a more severe, eremitic life and some important innovations were made but no major constitutional progress. The Italian ventures had their influence on France, but on the whole the Italian creations remained small bodies in their native mountains. North of the Alps the impulse came about 1050. It began with a shift to the eremitic life as in Italy, but the emergence of several religious leaders with a genius for organization produced a constitution type of great perfection. As several of the new orders spread all over Europe this constitution became the framework of a supra-national institute.

The new orders in Italy sprang from settlements made by men who had left the old monastic way of life in search of great simplicity, austerity, and solitude. The best known were the hermit-groups of Fonte Avellana and Camaldoli, and the communities of Vallombrosa. The two first owed their existence to St. Romuald of Ravenna (*c.* 950–1027), the third to St. John Gualbert of Florence (990–1073). Both saints had begun their religious lives as Cluniacs, and both had gone forth to become hermits, but while Romuald's foundations were groups of hermits, that of Vallombrosa followed the Benedictine Rule interpreted and extended in the direction of extreme austerity. Although the vocation to the eremitic life was spontaneous and authentic, it is certain that the reformers of the early eleventh century were aware of the teaching of the ancient Egyptian monks and modelled their lives upon the examples of the fathers of the desert. This revival of interest in the distant past was in part due to the influx into Italy of refugees from Asia Minor overrun by the Turks, and to the approach to Rome of a fervent Greek monachism from south Italy with St. Nilus at Grottaferrata, but it was also due to a new attitude to the literary memorials of the desert fathers, a seeking for ancient guidance, parallel to the contemporary research in the remains of ancient canon law. It was in direct imitation of Egypt, if not even as a kind of manifesto, that the settlement at Camaldoli was from the first called a 'desert'. That foundation on the mountainside near Arrezo consisted of a number of separate cells or hermitages within a wide enclosure. The monks lived in their cells and came together in the common oratory, refectory, and meeting-hall only at certain times and occasions. Later (1010) a second degree of the institute was established lower down the mountain with a monastery of common life following a strict interpretation of the Rule, from which experienced monks could pass to the eremitic life, as indeed St. Benedict had suggested.[1]

Camaldoli has a twofold significance in the history of religious orders:

(1) It was the first institute in which rules were drawn up for a group of hermits in the West, the first attempt to standardize and control what had hitherto been essentially free and unconfined. It was thus the prototype of a multitude of similar ventures of which the larger and more celebrated desert of La Chartreuse was the most notable member.

(2) It was the first religious institute embracing two kinds of life. This was to become, in one shape or another, a common phenomenon in the century that followed.

Vallombrosa, another mountain site, whose woods have been immortalized for English readers by Milton, had likewise a twofold significance.

(1) It was the first reforming monastery of the revival of the eleventh century in which the Rule of St. Benedict was officially interpreted in a strict sense, thus probably exceeding the severity intended by its author. Vallombrosa was therefore an anticipation, if not a forebear, of Tiron, Savigny, and the early Cistercians, and, centuries later, of La Trappe and the Primitive Cistercian revival of the nineteenth century.

(2) In order to free his monks from the distractions and

[1] *Regula* I. 3–5.

temptations of administration—then, as always, a source of trouble in the monastic life—John Gualbert added a class of non-clerical *conversi*, the class which in another form came to be known later as lay brothers. They did all the buying and selling and stewardship. This idea, as we shall see, was exploited with unhappy consequences by some of the northern orders, but adopted or adapted with triumphant success by the Cistercians and their imitators.

As the regularization of *conversi* added a new element to the monastic family, a word as to the origin of that institute may be in place, though no attempt will be made to discuss what is still a debated and obscure question.[1] The monastery of St. Benedict's Rule housed a community that was entirely homogeneous. Literate and illiterate, patricians and ex-serfs, all were there together on an exact equality, and the domestic and other menial and maintenance works were performed by all without discrimination. Ideal as such a scheme may be, the practical difficulties it encounters in any community that is not small in size and wholly remote from the ways and works of the world need no emphasis. Abandonment was inevitable when literacy and the occupations of literate men became universal in monasteries, and when to this was added the custom of monks proceeding to Holy Orders. The place of monks in menial as in agricultural work was taken by hired servants or serf labour, and it would seem that for several centuries no further development took place. In simple primitive houses the Rule was followed exactly; in large abbeys and their dependencies servants abounded. Then, in the early decades of the eleventh century, a class with different names and functions appears all over Europe, and at present it is impossible to decide whether or where the transmission of a practice takes place. This class of oblates, lay monks, bearded

[1] The long article of K. Hallinger, 'Woher kommen die Laienbrüdern' in *Analecta Sacri Ordinis Cisterciensis* (Rome, 1956), 1–104, is still the best general account. See also R. Duvernay, 'Cîteaux, Vallombreuse et Etienne Harding', in *Analecta Sacri Ordinis Cisterciensis* VIII. (1952), 379–404.

monks (*monachi barbati*) or converses (*conversi*) appears sometimes as made up of illiterate unordained monks, sometimes as of dedicated oblates, sometimes as of privileged servants, but it seems clear that their integration in the monastic order as a recognized body with a special function took place first at Vallombrosa, even if John Gualbert, as Hallinger suggests, took his idea from Cuxa in Spain.

The Italian ventures spread slowly and never had a resounding success. They catered indeed for the few rather than for the many and, in addition, they were racy of the soil of the wooded slopes of the Apennines. But they have continued to exist to the present day, and the desert of Camaldoli remains one of the most striking survivals in the mid-twentieth century of an institute peculiarly characteristic of the age of Peter Damian. Yet notable as were the Italian reforms, whose influence penetrated far and deep, if not widely, their place in European history is less significant than that of the northern bodies that came into being between 1050 and 1150.

In France as in Italy the first stirrings of new life showed themselves in a movement towards the hermit's life. The last half of the eleventh century in France saw the establishment of numberless hermits on the fringe of inhabited land. Normally, if the hermit was a man of exceptional gifts and reputation, he was joined by disciples who gradually formed themselves into an austere monastery. This, if it survived a few years, attracted many recruits and gifts of land and gradually reverted to type, becoming indistinguishable from its contemporaries. In England, Great Malvern and the whole new post-Conquest group of monasteries in County Durham and the East Riding of Yorkshire are examples.[1] Only very occasionally, as with Bruno of Rheims and his companions, the call to solitude was so strong and was followed so resolutely that it remained pure after the lapse of a generation. Bruno, indeed, laid the foundations of a celebrated institute almost unconsciously. Settling with some companions in the desolate uplands of the Grande Chartreuse, he formed in 1084 a colony like that of Camaldoli,

[1] *Monastic Order in England*, 160, 163–71.

which he may have imitated, as he may also have imitated Vallombrosa with his accompanying group of converses lower down the mountain. The hermits of the Chartreuse attracted good recruits and had a succession of able priors. They owed their permanent success to their resolute refusal, in early days as in late, to lower their standards and to tamper with their Rule in order to follow and fit the fashions of the day. They remained throughout the Middle Ages, and remain to this day, a spiritual élite, uncompromising and therefore few in number, but never degenerate and never extinct.

Their constitutional significance was to carry the work of Romuald at Camaldoli a stage further, to domesticate the eremitic life without destroying it. Though a drawing of a Carthusian monastery of the later Middle Ages is at first sight not remarkably unlike a house of any other order, it is in fact a Camaldolese desert cloistered and petrified. The scattered huts, the red-tiled cells, have become a row of miniature houses opening on a cloister. The life of the monks is not a whit less solitary, and the quarters of the lay brothers are segregated from the monks, even if, in late medieval foundations, they were often spatially not very distant.[1]

The Carthusians, however, were not destined to alter the face of monastic Europe. That was the work of a small group of men in a forest of Burgundy, some fifteen years after the settlement of Bruno at La Grande Chartreuse. This is not the place to rehearse the story of the foundation of Cîteaux, even though the tale told for eight hundred years has now, within the past three decades, taken a new form. Here we are concerned only with constitutional advances and reforms. What were the problems confronting reformers in the year 1100? Apart altogether from the moral and spiritual problems, experience and such knowledge of history as the monks of that age possessed pointed to two obstacles which had confronted and ultimately baffled reformers of the past.

[1] For the Carthusian constitution see Prior Guigo's *Consuetudines* in Migne, *P.L.* CLIII. 635 seq., and M. Thompson, *The Carthusian Order in England* (London, 1930).

First, the Rule of St. Benedict had become submerged under customs, some of which were legitimate interpretations while others were easy-going modifications, forming a jungle from which neither the individual monk nor the abbot of goodwill could escape. Secondly, there was a complete absence of any machinery or external authority to maintain or re-create a standard of observance. Hence any reform was personal and transient in its effects. Cluny had endeavoured to meet the problem without constitutional change by applying the abbot-subject relationship to the whole body of associated monasteries. Her period of success, which had been prolonged only by the exceptional merits and still more exceptional longevity of her abbots, was now about to end, for the new age had new demands for the monastic life. The need was now for a simple, austere life, and a framework to secure it. The epoch-making creation that was to supply this need rose unnoticed in the Burgundian woodland not far from Langres. There, a small group had resolved to break away from the conventional monastic life of Molesme and make a fresh and thorough start, with the watchword 'The Rule of St. Benedict to the last dot' (*Regula ad apicem literae*). They were led by two remarkable men, the prior Aubrey or Alberic and the superior Stephen Harding, a whilom monk of Sherborne who had sought and found his true vocation when returning from a pilgrimage to Rome. They settled in the forest of Cîteaux (1098) and Aubrey became abbot (1099–1109); he was succeeded by Stephen Harding (1109–34).[1]

The achievement of the first fathers of Cîteaux may be considered under two headings; the changes in the internal life of the monastery; and the new constitutional machinery. These correspond roughly with periods of time: the first with the years of Aubrey's rule, the second with those of Stephen Harding, and it is with the latter that we are concerned here.

[1] The English origins of Stephen Harding have recently been clarified by the discovery of a letter of his to the abbot of Sherborne; cf. 'An unpublished letter of St. Stephen', by H. Talbot, in *Collectanea Ordinis Cisterciensium Reformatorum*. III. (1936), 66–70.

IV

THE CISTERCIANS

THE early years at Cîteaux were difficult, and although recent scholarship has shown that neither numbers nor resources were as short as historians have generally believed, the fact remains that no foundation was made for seventeen years.[1] We know that the first fathers had discussed their problems and perhaps even formulated their programme long before leaving Molesme, and we may therefore suppose that the ruthless pruning of all the parasitic growth that had covered the rule was part of their programme from the beginning. On the other hand it has been argued with some probability that the 'puritanical', anti-aesthetical action which in the past was considered typically Cistercian, but which the *Exordium Parvum* specifically attributes to Abbot Stephen, was in fact due to the influence of the young Bernard, and that the campaign for plainness derived from Clairvaux, not from Cîteaux.[2] In any case it was not till 1113, when La Ferté, the first colony, was founded, that the great problem had to be faced. How were Cîteaux and her daughters to avoid going the way of all previous reforms? How was she to

[1] The origins and early constitutional history of Cîteaux have formed the centre of a vast hyperplasia of critical work in the past thirty years, and the last word has yet to be said. What follows in the text is, so it seems to the writer, a summary of points on which there is general agreement.

[2] Stephen became abbot in spring 1109; Bernard arrived probably in April 1112 (so J. B. Van Damme, 'Autour des Origines Cisterciences', reprinted from *Collectanea Ordinis Cisterciensium Reformatorum* (1958), 16–20, in the original 52–56. Granted (with Van Damme and J. Winandy, 'Les Origines de Cîteaux', in *Revue Bénédictine* LVII. (1957), 49–76, especially 63) that the tradition is reliable, that makes of Bernard's arrival with twenty-nine relatives the *momentum rerum* in the history of Cîteaux, it would seem very probable that the move towards 'puritanism' occurred after that event.

avoid decline without departing (as Cluny had departed) from the Benedictine conception of an abbot as the father of a single monastery? The answer, as it has come down the centuries, is given in the *Carta Caritatis*. Napoleon is credited with the observation that a constitution should be short and incomprehensible. Draftsmen in general have found the second quality easier of attainment than the first; the authors of the *Carta Caritatis* succeeded in producing a masterpiece of both clarity and brevity. In a document of some 1,600 words, a strong yet elastic framework was established which not only proved adequate for the immediate task, but adapted itself to conditions for which no precedent existed. Until very recently it was universally assumed that the *Carta Caritatis* was what it professed to be, a constitution drawn up possibly in 1112, certainly before 1114 (when it is mentioned in connection with the foundation of Pontigny), and approved by Pope Calixtus II in 1119. It was accepted as the work of Stephen Harding, who was in office from 1109 to 1132. As is familiar to all concerned with the twelfth century, the primitive documents of the Cistercians have recently been submerged in the acid bath of criticism, and have emerged with a new look. It has been shown conclusively that the *Carta*, as we have it in the later stereotype,[1] is the outcome of a long process, and early manuscripts give us glimpses of what that process must have been. Cîteaux had from the beginning resolved that any foundation was to be an abbey not a dependent cell. This was a direct declaration of principle as against the system of Cluny and Molesme, but it posed the great problem of the maintenance of discipline.

The stages of development have been discussed repeatedly in recent years as a result of the discovery of various forms of the *Carta Caritatis* that are clearly more primitive than the official stereotype, long familiar to all historians of the order in the form of the Cîteaux manuscript now in the municipal library of Dijon and printed by Guignard in his collection of

[1] i.e. the text of Dijon MS.601 of the Bibliothèque Municipale of Dijon, composed *c.* 1188.

Monuments primitifs de la règle cistercienne. Any discussion involves a comparison of many manuscripts and a decision on numerous points of dating, and a final scheme, recognized by all as certain, has not yet been agreed upon. A provisional reconstruction of the course of events would run after the following fashion, distinguishing four stages in the evolution of the *Carta Caritatis*. First, there was a short declaration of Stephen Harding, probably at the foundation of La Ferté in 1113. In this there were three clauses, written in the first person plural, in which the writer (Stephen Harding) promised that no material exactions would be made by Cîteaux, but that he retained responsibility for the souls of the daughter house. The Rule was to be observed there exactly as in the 'new monastery' (Cîteaux) and he insisted that all customs, books, &c., should be identical, so that monks from each house might be at home in the other. The next stage began when Pontigny was founded in 1114. This was the first house outside the diocese of Châlon, and it was imperative that the bishop should from the start give the monks freedom to follow their interpretation of the Rule; there is indeed a reference in the foundation charter to a *carta caritatis et unanimitatis*. Thenceforward there was a steady if gradual development, following a natural line of growth. At first the three (or four) abbots of the 'elder daughters' attended on a fixed day a chapter meeting at Cîteaux where they could accuse each other of faults of discipline and administration.[1] Later, the abbots held a chapter apart, the 'general chapter' of the order. Similarly, the relationship of surveillance and visitation existing between the abbot of Cîteaux and his daughters was applied to every founding abbot and his daughter houses. The third stage came after the death of Stephen Harding, when the routine of the visitation and abbatial election at Cîteaux,

[1] J. B. Van Damme, *Documenta pro Cisterciensis Ordinis Historiae ac Juris Collecta A* (Westmalle, 1959), 18. Illud tamen volumus nobisque retinemius, ut omnes abbates cunctarum partium illa die quam inter se constituerint, ad novum monasterium veniant, ibique abbati ejus loci et capitulo . . . obedient per omnia.

and the whole machinery of elections, were regulated. Finally, and probably not till about 1180, the practice was stereotyped in the form preserved in the official manuscript now at Dijon.

In other matters also we can watch the gradual development. In early days the bishop and canons of Châlon had the right and duty, as was laid down in the Rule of St. Benedict, to take cognizance of disorders and watch over abbatial elections. This relationship soon disappeared, and the order became autonomous, at first *de facto*, by the acceptance by the bishop of the *Carta Caritatis*, and later *de jure*, when exemption from episcopal control was standardized. In early days, also, the four elder daughters acted on occasion in concert with the abbot of Cîteaux and managed the mother house during an abbatial vacancy. These arrangements disappeared when the general chapter gradually became a sovereign body.

A similar development can be seen in the regulations governing the election and deposition of abbots. As a result of these findings the Cistercian constitution is seen to be the end-product of a series of decisions taken to meet new situations, and the *Carta Caritatis* as we have it is not a constitution given to the order by the first fathers, but a skilful summary of decisions that had been made successively. Consequently we need not look to Egypt for a model. It is true that the reformers of the eleventh century sought for precedents, and true also that the founding fathers of Cîteaux had possibly read the Rule of Pachomius and Jerome's account of Egyptian monachism. They must have known also that episcopal visitation of monasteries was prescribed by ancient canons, though these were now a dead letter. But all indications go to show that the clauses of the *Carta Caritatis* were devised to meet situations that arose; they were not the impositions of ancient practices. The very name of the document proclaims its age. The bond between Abbot Stephen and his first foundations was to be real and firm, but it was to be one of love—not the contractual, quasi-feudal bond of the charters that bound the monasteries to Cluny.

In the event, the two institutions of yearly visitation to secure the exact observance of a uniform code, and yearly general chapter for counsel, legislation, and judgement were found to be simple and effective measures that could hold together a widely scattered family of hundreds as successfully as it held together a group of half a dozen.

The body thus established was in a true sense, and for the first time in Europe, a religious order, a body of religious houses, scattered in different regions, linked together by legislation and disciplinary control, and based upon a focal point, the first mother, Cîteaux. It differed from the feudal, monarchical family of Cluny in two important respects. First it had no personal head, unaccountable to any body or code, such as was the abbot of Cluny. Cîteaux was the meeting-place of the abbots each year, because she was the beloved mother; but the abbot of Cîteaux had no more power and only a little more prestige than any other abbot. Actually there was an administrative débâcle at Cîteaux after St. Stephen, and for the next twenty years the abbot with the greatest moral power and initiative was the abbot of Clairvaux. Whether or not the decree of general chapter that no abbey was to hold a general chapter of its daughters was a glance in the direction of Bernard,[1] the *Carta Caritatis* held firm; Clairvaux remained one of the elder daughters, and no more. Secondly, there was no relationship of subordination of any abbot or abbey to Cîteaux or any other house. The autonomy of the individual abbey, and the stability of the individual monk, were complete.

Nevertheless, Cîteaux was not a fully developed religious order, for (i) It had no head to represent or direct it. (ii) It had no regional divisions; the lines of filiation ran across the

[1] *Ibid.* 'Ipsi vero [alii abbates] cum his quos genuerint, annuum capitulum non habebunt.' This has been seen by some as directed to the address of Clairvaux, the only house in early days with a numerous family, and by others as aimed at Morimond, when abbot Arnold was engaged in winning the support of his daughters to his eastern enterprise. It may, however, merely be an assertion that in this matter there is no duplication down the family tree.

Pyrenees, the Channel, and the North Sea. (iii) It was not strictly speaking supra-national, for no superior had any power to move a monk out of the abbey of his profession. It was in fact a half-way house between the Cluniac body and the international order. It was a federated body of equal and autonomous houses.

Besides their epoch-making constitutional machinery, the Cistercians, who prided themselves on their fidelity to the letter of the Rule, made two innovations which profoundly changed the character of the individual monastic family. Whether they realized how great these innovations were we do not know. So far as can be seen they did not either advertise or defend them; nor were they challenged by their adversaries. The two innovations were the abolition of infant oblation and the integration and exploitation of the lay brotherhood.

Infant oblation, that is the dedication of children by their parents in childhood to the religious life, was a practice far older than the Rule of St. Benedict, which assumes it as current.[1] In its original form it was soon to become repugnant to the feelings of western Europe, though it long survived in the milder form of receiving children for education with a view to encouraging personal dedication to the monastic life, and survived long in the Tridentine *petit séminaire* of Latin lands. The Cistercians' motive for abolishing it, which they never expressed officially, was presumably their resolve to have none in the monastery save those fully devoted to their life. By tacitly dropping the children they not only rid themselves of an element that must often have tended to laxity but they freed themselves of the necessity to teach boys and to develop their interest in grammar and literature. They also increased the spiritual importance of the novitiate and the master of novices. From being little more than a disciplinary overseer, he became a responsible formative influence and one required to give his judgement on vocations. As for the community, it now became a homogeneous body of adults all of

[1] For child oblation see *Benedicti Regula* LVIII.

whom had made probation and the decisive choice when at least sixteen years old.

Strangely enough, no evidence of any kind exists to tell us exactly when and where the Cistercians integrated the *conversi* into their system. There is no mention of them in the *Carta Caritatis*, whereas the *Usus Conversorum* presupposes their existence everywhere. Their institution is recorded in the *Exordium Parvum* with no indication of date.[1] We must suppose that the original intention that the monks, in St. Benedict's phrase, should live by the work of their hands, soon proved unworkable. Even when they had cut down their choir service to the minimum, the chanted office, sung Mass, chapter meeting, and the time of reading reduced the space for manual work to five hours a day (broken into two periods) on only four or five days a week, for feast days when reading took the place of work were numerous. Moreover, the five hours included getting to and from the scene of work twice, and the time spent in cleaning themselves and their tools. In the pioneering days, when they were making settlements in forest, heath, or moorland, or by swamp and river, heavy work at some distance from the abbey was essential. Even though they had allowed themselves from the beginning hired workers[2] (*mercenarii* but not serfs), the expense of these would have been prohibitive. They therefore evolved, almost by accident, the lay brother, a champion strain descended from the more primitive *monachi laici*, *monachi barbati*, and *conversi* of Hirsau and Vallombrosa, but nevertheless a wholly new type. Stephen Harding may have called in at Vallombrosa on his way to or from Rome, but we have no certainty of this. In any case, the early fathers devised for the white monks an economic instrument that for the time being was almost as influential as a mechanical reaper in enabling

[1] *Exordium Parvum*, ed. J. B. Van Damme, 13. 'Tuncque diffinerunt se conversos laicos barbatos licentia episcopi sui suscepturos, eosque in vita et morte excepto monachatu ut semetipsos tracturos.' The reason given is the supply of provisions, &c., for guests and the poor.

[2] Ibid.

them to bring new land under cultivation and surpass the manorial labour of feudal holdings. The converse-and-grange system, used all over Europe by the white monks and canons, was an innovation of major importance in the economic extension of the boundaries of cultivated land. It also attracted to the monastic life a great class hitherto excluded, the labourers and free peasants in an age of rising population. They responded to the call, literally in their thousands. The six hundred at Rievaulx were surpassed in many continental houses. Undeterred, the Cistercians prepared for them a home, a horarium, and a juridic status, *fratres sed non monachi*, and therefore lay brothers not monks.

V

TWELFTH-CENTURY DEVELOPMENTS

Cîteaux, like all successful organizations, had its immediate imitators. These may be divided into other monastic bodies in search of a formula, other religious groups irresistibly drawn into the fashion, and all other religious families which gradually adopted certain features of the Cistercian model.

Among contemporary monks may be noted the congregations of Tiron in Brittany[1] and Savigny in Maine.[2] Both of these were attempts to make a fresh start in monasticism and both were slightly posterior to Cîteaux, wherefore the marked resemblance in literal observance of the Rule, manual work, lay brethren, annual chapter and the like, may be supposed to be imitations of Cîteaux; they were certainly not its models. In the event Tiron went its own way and remained to the end of the Middle Ages a small peculiar congregation within the Benedictine family similar to that of the Olivetans. Savigny was better organized and became more popular, with a dozen houses in England, among them such well-known abbeys as Furness and Byland. It imitated the Cistercian life and constitution and formed an order of its own with an annual chapter. In time it was threatened with schism, especially in England, and in 1147 the abbot of Savigny threw himself and his family into the arms of the white monks, and they were merged without distinction in the family of Cîteaux.

Among those powerfully attracted must be mentioned the

[1] *Vita beati Bernardi Tironensis*, by Gaufridus Grossus, in *Acta Sanctorum*, April, II. 220 *seq.* (= *P.L.* CLXXII. 1367–1446). Cf. J. B. Mahn, *L'Ordre des cisterciens et son gouvernement* (2 ed., Paris, 1950), 29–34.

[2] *Vie de s. Vital par Etienne de Fougères*, ed. H. Sauvage, *Analecta Bollandiana* I. (1882), 355–90.

Norbertine canons or Premonstratensians. These religious followed the so-called Rule of St. Augustine, but Norbert, who had resisted persuasion to join the Cistercians, was nevertheless an admirer of the white monks, and a friend of St. Bernard. Consequently, when the first statutes were written (1131–4) they were largely based on the *Carta Caritatis* and the Cistercian Uses, and made of the white canons an order very similar in organization to that of Cîteaux,[1] though there were tensions present among the Premonstratensians that the Cistercians had not experienced. These were both internal, between the monastic and pastoral or apostolic trends, and external, between the members of the order to the east and to the west of the Rhine. Nevertheless, the Premonstratensians borrowed almost all the characteristic institutions of the white monks, such as general chapter, visitation, and lay brothers, and to a casual observer they were twins. There were, however, some small differences, introduced by chapter legislation. The practice of the Cistercians, outlined in the *Carta Caritatis*, that the abbot of a founding house should 'visit' his daughter yearly had been found awkward in practice when, for example, English abbeys made foundations in Scandinavia, but the white monks had been content with *ad hoc* remedies, empowering neighbouring abbots to deputize when needed. The Premonstratensians met the difficulty by appointing in chapter visitors for a regional circuit, called a *circary*. These soon became sub-divisions or provinces of the order, providing a model for the friars half a century later. At the summit, the abbot of Prémontré was something more than merely the president of the chapter. He was treated by all with special reverence and could at any time visit in person any abbey of the order.

Besides such immediate and wholesale borrowings, there were throughout the twelfth and early thirteenth century adaptations by other bodies of parts of the Cistercian constitution. Thus Cluny under the abbacy of Hugh V d'Anjou

[1] J. A. Lefèvre, 'À propos de la législation primitive de Prémontré' in *Annales Praemonstratenses* (1954), 12–19.

(1199–1207) adopted the annual general chapters of priors, who had, however, only a consultative voice. The Carthusians had begun to hold general chapters at irregular intervals from *c.* 1142, and in 1163–4 became an order on the Cistercian model.

In addition to the two new major orders of white monks and canons alongside the two original black orders, and the hermit-groups of the Carthusians, the twelfth century saw the rise of a whole crop of new religious institutes. Nothing shows the advance in ability to organize and administer between 1050 and 1150 more clearly than a comparison between the tentative arrangements at Camaldoli and the painfully detailed statutes of the Grandimontines or the Gilbertines. The former were founded near Limoges *c.* 1100 by Stephen of Muret, a hermit of noble birth, and removed to Grandmont in 1126. Though fully cenobitical under the Rule of St. Benedict, they were strictly contemplative, and their constitutions were marked by a note of extreme, not to say excessive, severity and poverty, with absolute silence and solitude, no possessions of any kind, and a perpetual ban against leaving their monastic enclosure. If abnegation and a code could ensure sanctity, the Grandimontines would have secured its presence. Their Rule breathes a spirit of rigidity and ferocity which anticipates some of the utterances of the fiercest Franciscan Spirituals or of Armand de Rancé of La Trappe.[1] One constitutional innovation is of interest. To safeguard seclusion the *conversi* were given not only the administration of the economy, as at Vallombrosa, but also the supreme responsibility; the monks were in fact their enclosed pensioners. This put a heavy strain on a weak link and ultimately led to a scandal, when the *conversi* rebelled and held the monks up to ransom for a better standard of living. In this matter history repeated itself. The Englishman, Gilbert of Sempringham, with an eye on Grandmont, gave his *conversi* complete control of the administration for his canons and

[1] The so-called *Regula S. Stephani* in *P.L.* CCIV. 1135–62 is not the work of the saint.

nuns. They proved unworthy of their trust, and under enterprising leadership embezzled funds and blackmailed Gilbert up and down England in hopes (which were in part realized) of an easier régime. With these precedents on record it is strange that St. Dominic, half a century later, should have proposed to give his lay brothers complete control of the temporalities—and comprehensible that his advisers should have vetoed the proposal.

Gilbert's own order was a response to the English version of the contemporary demand on the part of devout women all over Europe who lacked entrée to one of the aristocratic Benedictine houses or who had no nunnery in their neighbourhood. As under the conditions of the twelfth century it was useless to found a nunnery without an adjacent group of chaplains and confessors, the idea gained ground of establishing convents with a contiguous house of priests dedicated to its service and following a rule. Hence the so-called 'double' orders, which in fact differed in character from the double monasteries of the age of St. Hilda of Whitby.

The first of such ventures was made by the celebrated preacher Robert of Arbrissel,[1] who established the abbey of Fontevrault (1106) with nuns and lay sisters under the Benedictine rule, served spiritually and materially by himself and a community of priests. To modern eyes the peculiarity of this institute was that the abbess was its head, with jurisdiction over nuns and priests, the latter dedicating themselves to the service of the former, and receiving from them their livelihood. This system probably rose not of design, but from the circumstance that many of the nuns were nobly born and well dowered, while the priests were of humble origin and poor. Fontevrault soon became the most fashionable house in France for great ladies, and the abbess was often a princess of the blood; its English dependency, Amesbury, was equally fashionable; but as an order it was organized on Cluniac rather than Cistercian lines.

[1] *Vita b. Roberti*, by Baudry of Dol in *Acta SS. Februarii* III. 603–8, and *Extrema Conversatio b. Roberti*, ibid., 608 seq.

For us the significance of Fontevrault lies in the inspiration it provided for Gilbert of Sempringham, the founder of the only purely English order.[1] Gilbert, the priest of a Lincolnshire parish, with a genius for directing women, soon had on his hands a flourishing convent. Acting on Cistercian advice, he added lay sisters who, like the nuns, were to follow the Rule of St. Benedict, and later lay brothers following the Cistercian Uses to look after the farms.[2]

The nuns increased rapidly, and in 1147 Gilbert crossed to France with the hope of persuading the Cistercians to adopt his family. It was a bad year to choose, for it was that in which Savigny was added to Cistercian responsibility, and the fathers at that celebrated chapter, attended by Eugenius III, had enough on their hands. The Pope therefore ordered Gilbert to remain in charge, and inspired by Fontevrault he added a fourth class of canons, under the Rule of St. Augustine with some of the customs of Prémontré, to take care of the nuns, with himself as head of all, though as master, not as prior of Sempringham. Assisted by St. Bernard, he drew up an ingenious but exceeding prolix code laying down the plan of the two monasteries with all their offices, one on each side of a church with a double choir, together with elaborate regulations for separation and co-operation. The whole family was governed by a general chapter attended by the priors and cellarers and by the prioresses of all the convents, each with a companion. The rule or rules were a mosaic drawn from half a dozen different sources, but Gilbert had found and met a need, and his nuns were for more than a century numerous and fervent. Constitutionally regarded, Gilbert's family was less of an order than the Cistercians; it was a federation of Benedictine nunneries served by groups of

[1] The *Institutiones* of Gilbert are printed in Dugdale's *Monasticon Anglicanum* (ed. Caley, &c., 1830 printing) vol. VI. ii., as an intercalation between pp. 947 and 948.

[2] For this, see *Monastic Order in England*, p. 206, and for a fuller account of Gilbertine observance, Rose Graham, *Saint Gilbert of Sempringham and the Gilbertines* (London, 1901) and Raymonde Foreville, *Le livre de saint Gilbert de Sempringham* (Paris, 1943).

canons and lay brothers guided by a master. Its Rule was indeed an improvisation drawn up to fit an existing institute; its originality lay in the skill with which the various bodies were integrated. It had, however, what all the monastic and canonical orders had hitherto lacked, a single supreme head.

So had a totally different kind of order which had appeared shortly before the Gilbertines. The so-called military orders were, if not precisely the most characteristic institution of the Middle Ages, at least the one which could have originated and flourished in no centuries save the twelfth and thirteenth. The peculiar combination of the knight and the monk would have been unthinkable in the age of Charlemagne, and remained only as a name and a survival in the age of Chaucer. The two type-orders, which were imitated down the centuries in countries such as Esthonia, Spain, and Portugal, where wars called crusades continued, were the Knights of the Temple and the Hospitallers of St. John of Jerusalem.

The Hospitallers[1] were probably the earliest to appear. Beginning their career as keepers of a hostel for pilgrims in Jerusalem, they insensibly became wardens of hospitals and nurses of the sick. They adopted the Rule of St. Augustine and became a religious, non-clerical body; chaplains were added later. Outside their large hospital they were organized in small groups or 'commanderies'. The Templars[2] began in 1118 as a small group of knights pledged to defend the kingdom of Jerusalem, and were lodged by Baldwin II in his palace near the Temple enclosure. They prospered and sought the approval of the Church at the Synod of Troyes (1128). St. Bernard was present and at the height of his influence, and when the Templars appealed to him, he recommended the Rule of St. Benedict and the Cistercian Uses. On acceptance, they were given a white tunic (later bearing a red cross) and told to take the three monastic vows. They were ultimately

[1] For the Hospitallers, see J. Delaville Le Roulx, *Cartulaire général des Hospitaliers de S. Jean de Jerusalem* (Paris, 4 vols. 1894–1906).

[2] For the Templars, see H. de Curzon, *La Règle du Temple* (Soc. de l'histoire de France, Paris, 1886).

organized in three classes: knights, sergeants (*servientes*) of two kinds, men-at-arms and bailiffs and artizans, and chaplains. A fourth class of married knights was added as a kind of 'third order'. They lived, when outside their great crusading castles—castles without, monasteries within—in small groups in 'preceptories', and numerous English place names, Temple Balsall, Temple Cloud, Rothley Temple and the rest, are evidence of their brief stay.

Both orders were organized as military bodies with a hierarchy of officers—the supreme head, his adjutants-general, regional commanders, and local officers, and both rapidly lost their monastic character and became predominantly military. In both the knights alone were the governing class, and the whole order was ruled by the Grand Master of the Temple or the Grand Prior of the Hospital. Both orders also became extremely popular in England, France, and Spain, and gifts were showered upon them, with estates in remote parts of the land. To exploit these and collect their revenues posts were established all over Europe which acted also as recruiting offices for the castles and hospitals of the Levant. In the constitutional development of the religious order they are of importance in more than one respect. Firstly, their organization by regions and countries, divided into priories or bailiwicks and subdivided into commanderies and preceptories, was a new thing and served as a stage towards the provinces and custodies of the friars. Secondly, they were the first religious body to introduce the elective principle on a wide scale. The Grand Master and Grand Prior were chosen by an electoral committee appointed by a complicated system of election and co-option. Both orders indeed had general chapters, and the Templars also annual chapters in each priory, but the latter were attended only by the commanders of the other houses and the general chapter by the priors and any other invited by the Grand Master. As the Master appointed to all offices, the general chapter was to a large extent a meeting of his creatures, and though it had supreme legislative and corrective power it was in fact under the Master's control. Above all, the control of the whole great body by the Grand Master or Grand Prior was an important step towards the General of a religious order. Gilbert of Sempringham was the first to move in the direction towards which the Templars pointed.

Hitherto, nothing has been said of the influence of the papacy upon the constitutions of religious orders. The monastic movement never, even in Egypt, behaved as if it were independent of all Church authority, but in early times its seclusion and austerity separated it *ipso facto* from Christian society. Later, councils in the East, echoed by synods in the West, and, finally, imperial legislation gave to the bishop the right of visiting and controlling the monasteries within his sphere of influence, while recognizing that the monastic life as such was intangible. Whatever may have happened in the populous and civilized East, no active surveillance by bishops was customary in the West. The Rule of St. Benedict, and other contemporary Rules, presupposed the autonomy of an abbey and the absence of any regular supervision. The abbot presents an occasional subject for ordination, but otherwise the bishop is non-existent save as a witness to an abbatial election or as an authority to be called in by the neighbours if the monastery falls into a hopelessly bad way.

Gregory I, here, as in so many ways, an originator and a harbinger, was the first pope to defend the interests of a distant monastery, and the first case of canonical 'exemption' occurred shortly after, with the privilege to Bobbio issued by Honorius I in 628. We are not concerned with the history or pre-history of the fully implemented canonical exemption of the twelfth century. So far as individual black monk and black canon abbeys were concerned, exemption made no constitutional difference to their life, but the blanket exemption enjoyed by all the members of the Cluniac family naturally acted as a unifying and cohesive force. Cîteaux was in origin secured from interference by legatine protection and its own isolation, and Bernard a few years later made an eloquent, but somewhat unreal, protestation of the submission of the white monks to the normal rulers of the Church. In fact, the Cistercians were secure against interference by virtue of the *Carta Caritatis*. This, buttressed by papal approval, was presented to the local bishop by founding abbots, and once accepted rendered the new abbey virtually intangible, but in due course the whole order and that of the Premonstratensians became exempt. When the friars came, Francis, like Bernard, disclaimed exemption and wished his followers to work only if and where they found benevolent bishops, but such a status would have been in practice unworkable for a widespread active institute, and the four major orders of friars soon received exemption, subject to necessary reservations. From the middle of the thirteenth century, indeed, the organized religious orders became formally attached to the papacy. The friars in particular had direct contact with the Curia and a Cardinal Protector. As a direct consequence of this, the papacy began to exercise a direct control over the regulars in a way that would have been unthinkable a century earlier. The Fourth Lateran Council, by imposing regular general chapters and regular visitations upon the black monks and canons, took a first step towards creating of them a fully organized order, but conservative sentiment has down to the present day preserved these two great bodies from further regimentation, and the individual abbot is still canonically a *major superior* subject directly and solely to the Holy See.

Innocent III, however, was successful in imposing on the older orders some minor constitutional changes limiting the power of the abbot, which had been left without restriction by the Rule. Thus, while St. Benedict had required only the advice of the community on important issues, the Pope, and thenceforth canon law, made the consent of the chapter necessary for the reception of a novice and for major expenses and alterations. In part this was a reflection of the contemporary respect for collegiate powers, seen in the attention paid by canonists to the college of cardinals and the chapters of cathedrals. It was, perhaps, a salutary limitation on powers that had often been abused, and it has remained to the present day, as have smaller changes introduced by Benedict XII in 1336, but the process went no further, and abbots, with the Rule in hand, have never ceased to chafe at the necessity for obtaining a majority of votes on certain issues and by a natural reaction have been unwilling to listen to advice where constitutional consent was not needed. Speaking generally, the papacy has taken little part in the framing of religious rules and constitutions, and the endeavours of later popes to eliminate novelties from the Ignatian constitutions were never more than temporarily successful.

VI

THE FRIARS MINOR

DURING the first half of the twelfth century, and for fifty years more in the peripheral countries of Europe such as Scotland, Wales, Ireland, Scandinavia, and the eastern marches of the Baltic, the new orders of all kinds enjoyed a period of phenomenal growth. The Cistercians, first in time, were also easily first in numbers. Their vogue had been increased tenfold by the outstanding personality of St. Bernard, who dominated all ecclesiastical activities for thirty years, while at the same time acting as a most powerful magnet to draw all to Clairvaux. Indeed, it may fairly be held that although Bernard was in no sense the founder of the Cistercians, he did much to advertise the order and to wrest it out of its original groove of solitude and simplicity. By using it as a force in high church politics, and by giving an example of a Cistercian life of literary and preaching activity, he put an end for ever to the possibility that the white monks, like the Carthusians, might remain a silent, hidden, and austere body restricted to a small number by their severity of life. On the contrary, the general chapter was in 1153 constrained to pass a statute forbidding any further foundations save in exceptional circumstances. The total number of abbeys was then 330, of which no less than sixty had sprung from Clairvaux and her daughters. Within little more than fifty years of the foundation of Cîteaux the white monks had, so to say, saturated the old countries of Europe, and were to be found by riversides of Pembroke and Perthshire, by the fjords of Norway, in the forests of Sweden and among the marshes of Poland, within sight of the sierras of Spain, and among the mountains of Cyprus. Only a little, if at all, less spectacular was the diffusion of the white canons, especially in the great band of lowland country stretching from the towns of Flanders to the boundaries of Poland. But indeed every order, even including that of the original black monks, showed a marked increase during the century, and the benefactions of land and churches to them and to the military orders had been so great that a very large proportion, perhaps as much as a third of developed or exploitable land, was in the hands of the Church in one form or another, and the seeds of a great economic problem had already been sown.

At the same time, this popular surge towards the religious orders had its grave dangers. Not all those who joined even the stricter bodies had genuine vocations, while the new orders, by *c.* 1175 if not before, had compromised with the world around them and were receiving sources of income not permitted by their rules. Moreover, all the new orders were influenced by the climate of the age and catered for a feudal and agrarian society. The new urban, plebeian, mercantile elements, which were yearly growing stronger, were not represented among them.

Towards the end of the twelfth century a sense of lassitude and disintegration was creeping into the higher circles of church life. The monastic revival had spent its force, and the ingenuity of the constitution-makers had reached its limit. At the same time the Cistercians had given to the religious world three dynamic ideas: regular visitation, a legislative annual general chapter, and an organized lay brotherhood.

Meanwhile in the second half of the twelfth century an entirely new religious climate was developing in the towns of northern Italy and the valleys of the Rhine and Rhône, which were the first districts to profit by the new wealth and trade and the first to expand the weaving industry, which brought about the first industrial revolution in medieval Europe. In these centres of population, unaffected by the orders of monks and canons and imperfectly served by an ignorant and often degraded clergy, a new type of fervent lay piety made its appearance, containing almost from birth the germs of all the characteristics later associated with early Protestantism and Nonconformity: a distrust of sacerdotalism and sacramentalism, insistence on the reading of Scripture in the vernacular, zeal for preaching and hearing sermons, a love of association and 'meetings' for prayer, and the organization of charity. Of these the best-known and most permanent, if we exclude the frankly heterodox Albigenses, were the Waldenses of Lyons, who spread into Lombardy and south Germany, and the Humiliati of Milan and north Italy. Some of these became quasi-religious orders within the Church, others, like the Waldenses, gradually drifted into heresy.[1] For our purpose the interest of all these is the part they played in the pre-history of the friars, and we note in them: first the need of the urban population, both proletariat and bourgeoisie, for the devout life; secondly, the appeal of poverty and the communal life; and thirdly, the urge for moral exhortation and a study of the life of Christ, rather than liturgical prayer. It will be seen at once that the principal 'notes' of the friars' movement, preaching, mendicancy, and the invitation to the 'third' or 'penitential' order of lay people, correspond exactly to these needs. The rift, especially in Italy and Provence, between the official, moneyed Church, whether of high ecclesiastics or great religious corporations, and the masses of the people, whether well-to-do townspeople or illiterate peasantry, was growing yearly wider, and the threats to the sacerdotal and sacramental system foreshadowed a cleavage such as did in fact take place three hundred years later. Meanwhile the process was largely arrested during the pontificate of Innocent III by the rise of the two first orders of friars.

At the beginning of the thirteenth century it might have seemed, and did in fact seem to many, including the fathers of the Lateran Council, that there was no room for new religious orders. It was in fact one of the Lateran decrees, aimed presumably at the lay-preaching movement in Italy and France, that any groups in the future who applied for

[1] For all this, the fullest presentation is still that of H. Grundmann, *Die religiöse Bewegungen im Mittelalter* (Berlin, 1935; 3 ed. 1961); for more recent literature see Grundmann, 'Neue Beiträge zur Geschichte der religiösen Bewegungen', in *Archiv für Kulturgeschichte* 37 (1955), 129–82.

authorization should adopt an existing Rule, i.e. that of St. Benedict or St. Augustine. This decree, it would seem, was primarily the work of the numerous monks and canons who led public opinion at the council. It was not the personal view of Innocent III. That great pope had in fact a few years previously given his assent to a new brotherhood with a Rule of an entirely different character.

We are not here concerned with the personality of St. Francis, nor with the many and interesting critical problems that confront and perplex all who attempt to give an account of his life and teaching. For our purpose we have only to consider his order as and when it emerged from the mists of its origin into European daylight. Novel as was the order of the Friars Minor even when it had been combined and confined in the final Rule and had received the rubber stamp of the Curia, it was infinitely more original in its conception and first beginnings. Hitherto every new religious institute in the past two centuries had rested either on the code framed by its founder, or on a reformed version of an existing rule or constitution. St. Francis's aim was almost diametrically opposite. He did not wish to form a new order, but to get away, to cut loose, from all the traditions of the existing orders. Such an attitude could scarcely have existed in a mind trained in the ordinary school of medieval tradition, where *auctoritas* and law and the canons had such weight. Francis had never studied letters, and though very far from illiterate in the modern sense, he was always an outsider to the world of clerks and canonists and curialists. At the same time there was nothing of the rebel or the anarchist in his outlook. His originality is to be found rather in the circumstances of his conversion and vocation, in his own religious experience. Francis was taught by no one—by no man and by no book—he was turned from ordinary ways to the new life by the direct realization, or, as he would have said, by the direct and immediate vision and voice, of Christ in His human life and Passion. He was called to follow, not a way of life or a liturgical service, but a Person, and a Person who had a direct claim upon everyone else in the world. Consequently, once Francis had accepted the call for himself he was constrained to make it heard to others. He did not begin by wishing to found a monastery or a community; indeed it is probable that he never had such a wish in all his life, but he wished to live his new life with any brother in the whole world who might join him. It was his strong sense of the Church of Christ as an extension of Christ Himself that led him, when he had a dozen followers, to submit his way of life to the pope for approval. That was in 1209 and the pope was Innocent III. A short Rule was submitted; it has disappeared, but from references and from summaries in later versions it is clear that it consisted simply of a few key passages from the Gospels joined together by a short explanation. There was no question of a Rule in the ordinary sense, or of constitutions, for ten years more; and it is all but certain that Francis's thoughts continued to move along the lines of a small local group loosely bound together by mutual charity and a common vocation. Whatever his thoughts may have been, the ideas of simplicity, poverty, preaching, and mutual association were, as we have seen, in thick solution in the religious climate of the time, and only the least electric current was needed to precipitate them. The personality and sanctity of Francis supplied the shock, and recruits threw themselves at the saint and his companions. It was part of his humility and abhorrence of all prelacy that he should allow all dedicated friars to receive recruits to the body, and as a consequence their numbers could and did rise by geometrical progression. Nevertheless the genius and desires of Francis shrank from forming an institution or composing a code, and it was only in 1219, when divisions and extravagances began to appear, and when Francis himself, always ignoring, if not actually flouting, prudential considerations, left for the East without giving any date for his return, that ecclesiastical authority and ultimately the papacy moved in and applied to the Lesser Brethren some of the most elementary of the canonical rules governing all religious institutes, such as the year's novitiate, formal profession of vows, and local control of individuals.

Further increases in numbers and differences of opinion on policy, added to the difficulties caused by Francis's growing infirmities, led to a general demand for a Rule. This spelt the end of the free, homeless, penniless life of the roads and the hermitages, and Francis resisted at every stage. When at last he produced the so-called First Rule (*Regula Prima*) of 1221 there was widespread dissatisfaction; it was at once too exigent for the many and too imprecise for the canonist. It was written on the spiritual, not on the legislative level. Two years later after much mental anguish and possibly some sharp practice on the part of Brother Elias, a shorter and more commonplace edition was produced. This was the *Regula Bullata*, approved by Honorius III in 1223. When it began to bind them the Minors entered the ranks of the religious orders.[1]

The *Regula Bullata*, even with all the formalism that had been incorporated into it, was still something new. It is in fact the only new Rule between the Rule of St. Benedict and the Constitutions of St. Ignatius of Loyola. Leaving out of the reckoning the essential spiritual originality of St. Francis, the novelty of the Rule may be thought to be shown both in its internal, individual provisions and in the new kind of institute it created. The greatest novelty, even after all the canonists and conventional objectors had done their worst, was its spirit of freedom. All previous founders had led men away from the world and set before them life inside a monastery as the norm. Francis, though escaping in spirit from everything worldly as thoroughly as any Bernard, wished his friars to go about in the world working, reaching others and helping them.

Furthermore, in order that the friar might imitate Christ, his passage through the world must be unhampered by any possession of property. Hitherto and from the beginning, the individual monk had owned nothing, but the community as a unit owned property of every kind. Francis would never

[1] H. Böhmer, *Analekten zur Geschichte des Franziscus von Assisi* (2 ed., Tübingen, 1930) I, prints the *Regula Prima*, *Regula Bullata*, *Testamentum*, and Francis's letters.

allow his friars to own property either as persons or as a group; in his original conception they had neither land nor house nor chapel; they were to be always as were the apostles when sent to preach penance before the face of Christ. They were to live on what was given them for the spiritual or material work they did; failing that they were to live on charity and, in the last resort, to beg. Money, hard coin, was to Francis as something dirty and impure, and his friars were never to accept, keep, or even touch it. The insuperable difficulties in the way of holding to this idea, when numbers became large and when sickness, study, and the training of novices came in on the grand scale, will be obvious to everyone, and the attempts of Francis and later friars to resist relaxations, and the various shifts and changes on the part of well-meaning authority, are a recurrent and a distressing feature of subsequent Franciscan history. But however comprehensive the changes and concessions might be, the mendicant status of the Minors remained, and it was a new thing.

Constitutionally, there were equally important innovations.[1] First, the Minors were from their origin a family of indefinite size, not the community of a monastery or monasteries. When they grew numerous they were still one family with one head, Brother Francis. It was only when forced by necessity that Francis appointed lieutenants, called ministers or mothers, and later still divided their spheres of authority into wards and provinces. Consequently, while previous bodies, such as Cistercians or Premonstratensians, had been made up of

[1] The pioneer work on the Franciscan constitutions was the monumental article of F. Ehrle, 'Die ältesten Redactionen der Generalconstitutionen der Franziskanerordens', in *Archiv für Litteratur- und Kirchengeschichte* VI. 1–138, which still rewards any effort spent upon finding and reading it. P. Gratien's *Histoire de la fondation et de l'evolution de l'Ordre des Frères Mineurs au xiii*e *siècle* (Paris-Gembloux, 1928), though not wholly satisfactory on the course of events from Bonaventure onwards, has not been replaced by any book over the whole field. Fresh light has been thrown on the work of Haymo of Faversham and the relationship between the Dominican and Franciscan constitutions by Rosalind Brooke *Early Franciscan Government* (Cambridge, 1959).

monasteries with their communities grouped together, the Minors were a single family divided but not separated. They were indeed in origin something quite different from the monks and canons, and the conceptions of autonomy for the family and stability for the individual never entered into their composition. The friar belonged to his brotherhood, the brotherhood of Francis, and later to the body of Lesser Brethren, and when the order spread he lost his fatherland; any friar might go anywhere to do any work.

Seen from the other end, from the head, from the apex of the triangle, this placed new and unheard-of powers and resources at the command of the minister-general. Francis conceived his function as that of a super-servant waiting upon all his brethren, but it was not long before the servant became a satrap, and even a Bonaventure wielded and exploited immense power.

Finally the head of the brotherhood, largely through the geographical and other circumstances of Francis's life, was closely bound to the pope, his cardinals, and the Curia, and thus from the start the first centralized institute was based, not upon a mother house beyond the Alps, nor upon its head, wherever he might be, but upon Rome, and it was inevitable that in the sequel it should be used as an instrument by the papacy. All these tendencies were hastened by the concurrent development of the Friars Preachers. Nevertheless, we must not anticipate future changes. The Friars Minor, as established by Francis in the *Regula Bullata* and as persisting at least till 1239, were an unarticulated family, not a scientifically planned Order.

VII

THE ORDER OF PREACHERS

THOUGH twins at birth, and joined in a somewhat uneasy family relationship throughout the ages, the institutes of Francis and Dominic had neither a common origin nor a common design. Circumstances brought the two saints together, at first under Innocent III and then in a common atmosphere under the patronage of Cardinal Ugolino, later Gregory IX, but neither founder had imitated or influenced the other. Subsequently, however, the interaction was very great, though the historians of both orders make little mention of it. Put crudely and too simply, it has been said that the influence of the Minors made the Preachers into friars, and mendicants at that, while the influence of the Preachers made the Minors into an order, clerical and learned like themselves; but the borrowings and imitations if more subtle were also even more extensive than these general statements would suggest.

Superficially, the contrast between Dominic, the priest and trained theologian, the deliberate, far-seeing Spaniard, and Francis, the unlettered, impulsive Italian is great, and has often been stressed and overstressed. Dominic had begun his priestly life as a secular canon; his chapter had subsequently reformed itself under the rule of St. Augustine, with customs taken from Prémontré. He had followed his bishop on a missionary expedition to Denmark, but with him had been diverted to the Albigensian heretics of Languedoc. Here he had gathered round him a group of preaching companions. He and they realized, what had been felt by many since the days of St. Norbert, that the prime external need of the Church was for a thoroughly trained body of preachers, ready to counteract heresy and ignorance and to exploit the vast new store of theological learning accumulating in the schools.[1] In 1215 Innocent III told Dominic to choose a Rule and constitutions for his institute and present them for approval at Rome. The Lateran Council had just decreed that new institutes must take an old Rule, and Dominic as a regular canon naturally chose the Rule of St. Augustine as his basis, and it was his intention at first to establish a canonical body. The pull of the Minors was, however, too strong. The two saints are said to have met in Rome (in 1217 or 1221), and St. Dominic is alleged to have proposed a merger of their followers under Francis's leadership.[2] Francis, so the story runs, refused, but a few years later, in 1220, the Preachers relinquished all income from rents and revenues which they had retained in 1216, and adopted the strict corporate poverty of the mendicants. Meanwhile Dominic had composed the code governing the domestic life of his followers, the so-called First Distinction of the Constitutions.[3]

In this no individual element was new. The life of the brethren in their convents, which were from the first, in contrast to the early wishes of Francis, regarded as the essential *points d'appui* for the whole order, was to be strictly monastic in character, and Dominic drew several of his provisions from the Uses of Prémontré. The originality lay in the adaptation of the monastic life to the ruling purpose of the friars, which was doctrinal preaching. Every priory was to be a house of

[1] P. Mandonnet, *S. Dominique; l'idée, l'homme et l'œuvre*, ed. M. H. Vicaire (Paris, 1938) and Père Vicaire's great biography, *Histoire de S. Dominique* (Paris, 1957; Engl trans. London, 1964).

[2] Vicaire and Dominican writers in general regard the meeting as legendary, but there is some evidence and considerable probability in favour of its historicity; see *The Religious Orders in England* (Cambridge, 1948) p. 149, n. 5, and Vicaire, *S. Dominique*, p. 494, n. 41 (Eng. trans.).

[3] H. Denifle's two articles, 'Die Constitutionen des Prediger-Ordens von J.1228' and 'Die Constitutionen des Predigerordens in der Redaction Raimuns von Penafort', in *Archiv. f. Litt. u. Kirchengeschichte* I. 165–227 and V.530–64, are masterpieces of critical and analytical skill, and have not been replaced. There is, however, the full and excellent survey of G. R. Galbraith, *The Constitution of the Dominican Order, 1216–1360* (Manchester, 1925).

study and training, and all observance was modified when that end demanded it. The liturgy was shortened and attendance at choir and the observation of strict fasting might be dispensed in the interests of study. Each priory was to contain a master of theology, and the order soon built up a European network of *studia particularia* (houses of study) for each province and of *studia generalia* (international houses) for the ablest minds of the whole order; these latter were for the most part at university towns such as Bologna, Paris, and Oxford.

The arrangements within the friaries, however, did not of themselves affect the constitution of the order. This was achieved with signal success in the Second Distinction of the Constitutions, which was not finally confirmed until the chapter of 1228 though it had been observed for some years, perhaps even in Dominic's lifetime (he died in 1221). Whether it was wholly the work of Dominic himself or principally devised by some of the Bolognese masters who had joined him is uncertain, and in a sense immaterial, since it was almost certainly composed during his mastership. It was in effect a most carefully framed system, in which the supreme legislative and administrative powers were given to boards, of whom the majority, over the years, were elected directly and were not office-holders, while the others, though officials, owed their position to a previous election. The advantages of firm government and of representative wisdom were thus combined. The Dominican organization has been described as a democratic constitution and as an essay in representative government, but in fact the object of the founder was not to ensure that the voice of the majority or the opinions of various sections should be heard or should prevail, but that in an order of trained clerics supreme power should reside with a council of representative wisdom, rather than with a chapter of prelates holding office for life or with a junta of corps commanders.

The order was divided into provinces, and the provinces were made up of priories. Each house had its prior, elected domestically by the resident community; each province its provincial prior, elected by a prior and a delegate from each priory; over the whole order was a master-general, elected by the priors-provincial and two representatives from each province. On each level there was a chapter differing widely in numbers, procedure, and powers. At the conventual chapter all took part, save for minor restrictions in elections. The provincial chapter was very large. Each priory sent its prior and a representative, and preachers-general attended *ex-officio*. This would mean almost 200 members for the English provincial chapter. The whole chapter, however, functioned as a body only to elect a representative (*diffinitor*) for general chapter and four *diffinitors* from among its numbers who, under the chairmanship of the provincial, performed all the business of the chapter, which was ratified at a plenary session. The provincial prior held office until he died, resigned, or was 'absolved' in general chapter. He was elected by a large body, some 300 strong in England, of the priors and two delegates from every priory. The master general of the whole order was elected by the prior provincial and an elected *diffinitor* from each province. His was in effect a life office, save for resignation, but the master was technically amenable to general chapter when this was in session.

The provincial and general chapters were held annually, and the latter ran in cycles of three. For two years the capitular body was composed of elected delegates (*diffinitores*), in the third, of provincial priors, and no legislation could take effect till it had passed three chapters.[1] Between the chapters at each level the government was conducted by the master and the provincials and conventual priors, but the sovereign power was always the general chapter.

In another way also the Second Distinction was revolutionary. It broke away entirely from what may be called the

[1] Dominic also made provision for a *capitulum generalissimum*, made up of master-general, priors provincial, and provincial delegates, which could be summoned on general demand and which could pass legislation at once, but there were only two such chapters in the Middle Ages, both in early times, 1228 and 1236.

monarchic or hieratic or paternal conception of power. The monastic (or canonical) abbot was elected for life and solemnly blessed; as abbot he stood in the place of Christ and received external, distinctive honour; even if he resigned he retained his rank and certain privileges; his tomb was in a place apart and if he were ever canonized he had a special Mass in the Missal. The Dominican priors and provincials, on the other hand, and even the master general, were regarded as brethren, in authority indeed but still brethren, and when they ceased to rule they became once more simple friars. On the other hand a friar who had never held office might, as diffinitor in chapter, initiate legislation for the whole province or order, and at two out of every three general chapters, as has been seen, the elected diffinitors were in a majority. Proceedings in the three chapters were governed by complicated but wholly sensible regulations which covered every eventuality, and it is a tribute to the genius of Dominic and his helpers that the machinery established in 1220–8 should have functioned smoothly and essentially unchanged from that day to this. Its superiority as a clear and practical document stands out at once if it is compared with the cumbrous, disordered regulations of the Gilbertines. Combining as it did some of the best elements of canon law and civic practice, the Dominican constitution served in its turn as a model for cities and associations in search of a code, while in its main lines it was adopted by the other bodies of friars, and has influenced almost all subsequent religious orders. With the Dominicans, indeed, the complete supranational religious order, at once fully centralized and fully articulated, had achieved adult stature, and in most ways the model could not be bettered.

The Dominican constitutions were probably in force before the death of St. Dominic in 1221. At that date and for long after the Friars Minor were in no such settled condition. At their head from 1232 to 1239 was a minister-general possessing powers undefined and in the founder's intention beneficent, but in practice absolute and potentially despotic, as the later years of Elias showed. The general assembly, again of undefined composition and competence, but containing certainly all the ministers-provincial, the creatures of the general, could only meet when summoned by their chief, who, like King Charles I, could dispense with meetings if, with Brother Elias, he preferred personal rule. Meanwhile the general, in whose hands lay the appointment of the provincials, could of his own free choice divide, amalgamate, or add provinces. The only code was the *Regula Bullata* of 1223 and a few resolutions of questionable canonical validity passed in general assembly.

It was while things stood thus that Brother Elias, himself an educated man though not in Holy Orders, succeeded with the support of a majority of the provincial ministers in converting the Minors decisively into a clerical and a learned body, with the necessary corollary of fixed urban convents. They thus became indistinguishable in their work and life from the Preachers, but their constitutional position was very different and remained unsatisfactory, especially in the eyes of the university-trained masters who were now the order's strength, and the inevitable crisis was precipitated by the autocratic and finally scandalous behaviour of Brother Elias. He was deposed in 1239, but in the weeks that preceded the chapter in Rome at which the deposition took place a committee of the reformers had drawn up a comprehensive set of constitutions with the twofold purpose of preventing the emergence of a second Elias and of providing the organization needed by a learned and clerical body of friars. The leading spirit was the Englishman Haymo of Faversham, who became minister-general only a few months later, succeeding the short-lived Albert of Pisa (1239–40). Haymo, a secular master of Paris till 1226, was a personal friend of the second master-general of the Dominicans, Jordan of Saxony, and a recent historian has judged that 'he would have made an ideal Dominican'.[1] It was inevitable that he and his colleagues should look to the Dominican constitutions as their model, and though recent research has modified the previously current view that the Franciscan constitution was all but a

[1] G. R. Galbraith, op. cit., p. 203.

replica of that of the Preachers,[1] it remains true that in the matter of organization and government, as also in the regulations for the studies of the order, the Minors adopted most of the key principles of the Preachers, and in particular the regularization of general and provincial chapters and the introduction of the elective element.

Nevertheless the Minors, after experiments in the years 1239–44, ended by retaining important elements of the early spirit of the order. Thus their general chapter, though now regular and compulsory, was triennial, not annual, and had always the same composition, viz. the provincial, one custodian, and one elected member for each province; as there were more provinces in the order than the Preachers had, the general chapter was larger and the official representation greater.

Similarly, though the general chapter was in principle sovereign, its relative infrequency and all the tradition of the order gave the effective power to the minister-general and his provincials. We may say that the Franciscan order was a constitutional monarchy, whereas the Dominican order was a firmly governed republic.

The success of the first two orders of friars, which was even more spectacular and widespread than that of the Cistercians a century earlier, inevitably provoked imitation, and their organization acted as a transformer for existing bodies. Two of these deserve mention, since they ultimately rose to something like parity with the Minors and Preachers. The first was the hermit congregation that blossomed into the order of Our Lady of Mount Carmel. They came first into sight on the slopes of Carmel *c.* 1140, and about 1210 received a Rule or directory, not unlike that of the Camaldolese, from the patriarch of Jerusalem, St. Albert of Vercelli, and split up into several groups. About 1238 they were dislodged by the

[1] R. B. Brooke remarks (*Early Franciscan Government*, p. 226) with considerable reserve: 'The result [of comparing the constitutions] is not perhaps quite what we might have expected. The extent of Dominican influence is not particularly impressive.' Mrs. Brooke analyses the relationship in detail, ibid., Appendix III., pp. 293–6.

Saracens and migrated separately to Cyprus, Sicily, and Europe. Among the first to reach the West were a party who were established near Alnwick, while another colony settled in the Weald of Kent, and from this circumstance the English province had great weight in the first decades of its existence in Europe. The Carmelites were at first faithful to their hermit vocation, but the European recruits knew nothing of Carmel, and the pull of the friars was too strong to be resisted. At a general chapter held at the middle of the century in London the whole orientation of the order was changed by obtaining certain mitigations from Rome, including permission to settle in towns; settlements were forthwith made at Cambridge and Oxford and constitutions were adopted similar to those of the Preachers, though with a few interesting variations.[1] The fourth order, that of the Augustinian hermits or friars, was unique in that it was created as an order by a papal act of power. A number of congregations of hermits in Italy, who had adopted the Rule of St. Augustine and had imitated the way of life of the early Minors, were causing confusion to themselves and others. Innocent IV united several groups, and in 1256 his successor, Alexander IV, united them all as the Hermits of St. Augustine with the status of mendicant friars. They adopted in time the Dominican organization in all its essentials, and indeed imitated the Dominicans very closely in their emphasis on theology and preaching.[2]

Besides the Carmelites and Austin friars the mid-thirteenth century saw the rise of a number of mushroom and splinter orders of friars. In the strong reaction of the secular clergy to the mendicants, both at the universities and in the parishes, which attained its peak of energy *c.* 1260–75, a resolute attempt was made, culminating in a frontal attack at the Council of Lyons in 1274, to abolish all the friars save the first two orders.

[1] They have been studied by Fr. Keith Egan, O. Carm., in an unpublished Ph.D. thesis in Cambridge University Library, 'The Carmelite Order in England' (1965).

[2] Several articles on early Augustinian history are in *Analecta Augustiniana*.

The Carmelites escaped with difficulty, and the Austin Hermits with more difficulty still, but all the others were scheduled for suppression, though some maintained an underground existence for many years, and others, like the Crutched Friars, escaped by slipping a few yards over the frontier dividing them from the regular canons. Only one more order of importance was born in the second half of the thirteenth century, the Florentine order of the Servites, which followed the prevailing fashion and became mendicant.

With the friars the religious order attained administrative perfection. A vast body of men, contained within an elastic framework and organized by a skilful combination of egalitarian opportunities, elected merit, and authoritative direction, could be deployed upon or directed towards any work that the supreme council considered desirable, while the head of all was in close touch with the head of the universal Church, protected by papal support and used for papal needs.

Seen from another angle, the Dominican order appears almost as an example of biological evolution from the monastery of Monte Cassino. The simple body becomes a complex organization which has developed organs and powers in response to needs and environment, while species less fully developed remain in existence to witness the stages of the progress, and certain organs and functions have disappeared as useless. Seen from yet another angle, the complication of the machine has to some extent replaced the variety of individual needs as the object of attention. The chapters and officers are more concerned with running the organization than with caring for the individual. An historian of the Dominicans observes that 'the Founder of the Order of Preachers was not primarily interested in the souls of his followers.... He thought of them as dogs—dogs [*Domini canes*] to drive back into the fold those sheep who were wandering to destruction.'[1] This judgement would no doubt have been warmly combated by St. Dominic and his sons, and it is certainly true that the worth and work of an apostle and a preacher is in exact relation to his

[1] G. R. Galbraith, op. cit., p. 7.

own love of God. *Nemo dat quod non habet*; and the friar who neglects his own soul will not save another's. St. Dominic composed the First Distinction for his friars as well as for their work. Nevertheless there is a truth in the judgement just quoted; in a Cistercian monastery the abbot exists to teach and guide his monks in the ways of Christian perfection. Their first duty is to love and praise God apart from the world; they love their neighbour by mutual charity and by intercession and it may be by example. In a fully organized 'active' order the visible effort of all should be directed to the spiritual work of the order, and the function of the official is to direct, exhort, and organize to that end, convinced that the work, rightly done, will sanctify the doer.

Finally, in the process of development, much of the external monastic life has disappeared. The solemn liturgy, the processions and litanies, much of the silence, fasting, and retirement, the monastic enclosure, all these have gone or have been reduced to a minimum. St. Francis had originally hoped to escape from all the external regulations of monasticism, not because he despised the monastic ideal but because his way was the way of simplicity, the love of Christ without ways and means. St. Dominic, by vocation a regular canon, relinquished some observances to win time for study. In the event the friars remained within the direct line of development from the monastery, and it is not without reason that in French and some other languages they are alluded to as monks (*moines*). The complete break did not occur till the sixteenth century.

VIII
TRANSITION TO THE MODERN WORLD

OUR survey might well have ended with the friars. With them the medieval development of monastic organization reached its term. Yet the Society of Jesus, that tremendous force in the Counter Reformation, deserves notice as being in many ways a still further stage in the de-monachization of the religious life, while in other ways it was an advance even upon the Dominican constitution in centralization and efficiency. Similarly, the Benedictine reform known by the name of its leading abbey, Santa Giustina di Padova, is significant as providing a model for many future congregations. As with so many of the intellectual and practical innovations of the first age of what is called the modern world, there is a mixture in both these institutes of acceptance from the previous age of its machinery and of neglect of the germinal ideas of the past. In both cases the organization of the friars is clearly admired and in some respects imitated, while the mainspring of the monastic institute, the paternal and spiritual quality of the abbatial office, is modified or abandoned.

Santa Giustina of Padua

Among the external causes of monastic decadence from the eighth to the fifteenth centuries none had been more universal or more harmful than the practice of 'commending' the office of abbot to one who was not a member of the community or order concerned. In Carolingian times it had been a component part of the system of lay ownership of churches (*Eigenkirchentum*) and its worst features of ownership and spoliation had disappeared in the general reform of the eleventh century.

It continued, nevertheless, as a canonical expedient and was used increasingly by popes to provide a livelihood or rewards for officials and dignitaries, and in the later Middle Ages was practised also by the kings of France and Spain, who by custom or concordat had gained control of the higher patronage of the Church in their dominions, and distributed the spoils to laymen, women, children, and even (in post-Reformation France) to Protestants. Besides its often disastrous economic effects, *commendam* had the deeper spiritual consequence of eliminating the keystone of the monastic community, the abbot, the one person set apart from the rest by the Rule as governor and teacher with the care of all things temporal and spiritual. Doubtless in other orders and in some phases of monastic history (e.g. in the Cluniac system or in English cathedral priories) a superior without the rank of abbot had succeeded in ruling a community with spiritual and temporal success, but speaking generally, in the case of large and autonomous Benedictine houses the practice was baneful. It usually implied the appointment of a prior by an external agent, and a drastic curtailment of his religious and economic initiative. At the very least it gave an unreality to much of the teaching of the Rule and deprived the acting superior both of the moral support and urgent sense of responsibility given by the traditional office of abbot. An original and effective remedy was found in Italy at the beginning of the fifteenth century.

Ludovico Barbo, a Venetian, placed by Gregory XII as abbot of the decayed monastery of Santa Giustina at Padua, had for some twenty years (1408–31) fostered and ruled a reformed community and made of it the nucleus of a congregation.[1] *Commendam* was to be by-passed by a system of dependent priories, and later by the institution of a general chapter of abbots and priors under the abbot of St. Giustina as the sovereign authority, appointing all subordinate superiors. Difficulties arose, and the matter was settled in 1432 by Eugenius IV, an old friend and confrère of Barbo, by a completely new arrangement. Life-abbots were to disappear even

[1] I. Tassi, *Ludovico Barbo, 1381–1443* (Rome, 1952).

at Santa Giustina; all monks were to belong to the congregation, not to the house; abbots were appointed for a short term and if successful were moved round the houses. The sovereign power was the annual general chapter (an abbot and a delegate from each house) but in practice it lay with its committee of *definitors* (cf. the Dominican system) of nine, who performed all the executive, legislative, and elective functions of an abbot or chapter and elected visitors to enforce discipline and legislation between chapters. It is an interesting reflection in the monastic world of the government by council and by committee that had found so many advocates in the 'conciliar epoch'. Though radical and frankly anti-traditional, it succeeded in its first purpose of reform, and Santa Giustina was a focus of ardent monastic life for more than a century. The system was imitated by Monte Cassino and its allies, and by the congregation of Valladolid in Spain. With slight modification it lay behind the great congregations of St. Vannes and St. Maur in seventeenth-century France. It was adopted in part by the revived English congregation in the same century, and endured in the English houses until 1899. It was again adopted in part by the reformed congregation of Subiaco in the mid-nineteenth century. In all these cases it gave temporary or lasting benefits, but it was inevitable that sooner or later, when *commendam* went for ever at the French Revolution, a return should be made to the traditional autonomous monastery ruled by an independent abbot, and during the past century Benedictines all over the world have moved in this direction. Santa Giustina nevertheless remains in monastic history as a successful and lasting reform before the Reformation, and one which straddled the tormented sixteenth century to bear fruit in the post-Tridentine Church.

The Jesuits

The Jesuits stand with a foot in each of two eras, the medieval and the modern, partly because while they were in a true sense heirs and products of the medieval tradition, they are also the great revolutionaries. They are the last word, the *ne plus ultra*, in the organization of the religious order, while they go further than the friars in shedding the traditional monastic character of claustral life and liturgical prayer. In the early years of the sixteenth century it might have seemed that the religious order had no future. Its principles had been attacked by the Reformers, and many of its practices, attacked by humanists, Erasmians and Lutherans alike, seemed on the point of disappearance in the collegiate establishments and the associations of clerics of the fifteenth and early sixteenth centuries. Seen in this climate of ideas, the Jesuits may be said to have saved the religious order for the church militant. From them almost all the orders and congregations of active life in the post-Tridentine world took their shape.

The first Parisian group of the Company, seven in number, took their vows on Montmartre on 15 August 1534, when Sir Thomas More was already in the Tower. They received their first papal authorization in 1540. Before that, Ignatius and five others had with prayer, hard thinking, and much debate, produced five articles as a basis for papal approval. These, containing in a few words what were to remain the main points of the Constitutions, were in brief as follows:

(1) The aim of the Society of Jesus is to preach the faith, engage in works of charity, and in particular to instruct children and the simple, under complete submission to the decision of the superior of the Society.

(2) The members of the Society, both its superior and all others, are to be absolutely at the disposal of the Pope.

(3) They are to recognize and honour the superior as Christ, and he is to treat them in Christlike love.

(4) Absolute poverty, personal and corporate, is to be observed by the professed save in the case of houses of study.

(5) The choral office is relinquished and the wish is expressed to abandon also chant and music of all kinds, and to adopt no peculiar habit.

Ignatius began his consideration of the full Constitutions in

1544 and worked upon them with intensity in 1548–51. They were then revised by some of the Fathers in Rome and subsequently issued experimentally. They were not finally approved by the Pope till 1558, two years after Ignatius's death. An autograph of the founder's final version exists, and there is general agreement among both scholars and Jesuits that in their totality the Constitutions are his work, built upon the deliberations of earlier years and the labour and experience of later ones. They are in essence still the law of the Society. Though there is a logical order in them, the skeleton of government has to be picked out here and there from among other regulations.

The Society was composed of several classes, which are enumerated in various ways by different writers. Regarded as a body in existence at a given moment, the Society is made up of unprofessed novices; scholastics professed in private simple vows, which can be terminated by authority at any time; temporal coadjutors professed in simple vows; spiritual coadjutors in Holy Orders, professed in simple vows taken publicly but dispensable under certain circumstances; and priests professed in solemn vows binding themselves to the Society and the Society to them in perpetuity: in all, five classes.

For individuals passing through the career, the process is as follows. The postulant for admission is received into the novitiate without formal assurance of his future classification. After a year's novitiate he may be destined for temporal coadjutorship, whereupon he takes in private simple vows and enters at once upon his life of active service on a level corresponding to his abilities, from simple manual or domestic work to highly skilled secretarial or typographical and other craft employment. If he is selected for the spiritual coadjutorship he makes a second year's novitiate, after which he enters the scholasticate, and for some ten to twelve years completes his secular studies at university or training college level, and passes through the normal course of philosophical and theological study. Before his theology he normally spends two or three years teaching classes at one of the Society's schools. When his theology is complete he is ordained priest and passes through a third year's novitiate or 'tertianship'; after which he becomes either a spiritual coadjutor or a fully professed member. In the latter case he adds to the three vows of religion additional undertakings to go into the mission field whenever and wherever the Pope may decide, and not to solicit or to accept ecclesiastical preferment, save at the direct command of the Pope. This last class of solemnly professed alone are eligible for the highest positions in the Society, such as the generalate, provincialate, and assistantships to both, but non-professed fathers can be rectors of colleges, heads of houses, and leaders of missions.

Three features of this division are noteworthy as original: the allotment by authority of the career to be pursued at each moment of decision; the allocation of class by an examination of natural, physical, psychological and intellectual qualifications (assuming a basic spiritual qualification in all); and the existence of a small governing class which reminds us (though surely not Ignatius) of the ruling class of Plato's Republic, to which indeed there is more than one resemblance in the constitution of the Society. In the traditional monasticism all postulants were received for membership of a single undifferentiated community; when lay brothers were integrated at Cîteaux they chose the life with a separate régime, while even among the friars all clerical members of the order had full and equal 'political' rights. In no case was there an oligarchy of talent.

The Company, in fact, was regarded by Ignatius as a chosen body of active talents rather than as a home or haven for those seeking primarily the individual service of God apart from the world. Hence all were put through a searching examination before admission, and then and at every later stage of decision intelligence, good judgement, good health, and a strong constitution were taken seriously into account, in addition to the moral and spiritual qualities of the aspirant. At least to some extent, the fully professed are chosen from the others by an assessment of qualities similar to that which would govern the choice of a Fellow of a college from among a group of candidates who were schoolmasters. How far this bias in favour of mental or intellectual qualification was primitive in the Society, how far it was due to the experience of Ignatius, who came the hard way up to learning, how far it was due to the acknowledged shift of the basic purpose of the Society from elementary apostolic work to advanced educational direction, are questions which do not concern us, but we may note also that the Society from the beginning retained powers of summary dismissal wider than those in other orders. With the others, a graded series of severe physical punishments and imprisonment had to be shown to have been useless before final dismissal. When Ignatius, so the story goes, was asked where he kept the prison for the disobedient, he pointed to the door.

The constitution of the Society, as seen in the Constitutions,[1] is strictly authoritarian and monarchical. It bears indeed a very close resemblance to that of the Church under the fully developed papacy of the thirteenth century. At the head is a general, elected for life, unaccountable to any person or body for any act of his administration, removable only for heresy or for gravely sinful and scandalous conduct. He is elected in a general congregation, which consists of the provincials and two elected representatives from each province, by a clear majority of the members, or failing this by a majority in a small committee of three or five electors. Apart from the meeting at a demise of the generalship, the general alone can summon a general congregation, and he is specifically discouraged from doing so by the Ignatian Constitutions, on the grounds that it will take up people's time unnecessarily.[2] As a matter of history, extraordinary general congregations

[1] Quotations are from the critical edition of the Constitutions in *Monumenta Historica Societatis Jesu*, vol. 65: *Monumenta Ignatiana*, ser. 3. *S. Ignatii de Loyola Constitutiones Societatis Jesu* III (Rome, 1938).

[2] *Constitutions*, P. viii, ch. ii, 226. Illud in primis suppositum sit quod non videtur in Deo in præsentiarum expedire ut certis temporibus

have been almost as rare as *capitula generalissima* among the Dominicans. In any case the general is not bound by congregational decisions. He cannot, however, change the constitutions or decrees, though he may dispense with himself and others in regard to their observance—a remarkable, wise, and original provision which has worked well in practice though never, it would seem, imitated by secular legislators.[1] The general appoints the provincials, rectors of colleges, superiors of the houses of professed, and novice masters, and has constitutionally complete and immediate control of the status and movements of all his subjects. He is provided with a small group of assistants (originally four in number) elected by the general congregation for life, each of whom makes himself expert on the affairs of a group of provinces and advises (but cannot control) the general. He also has with him a monitor, usually his confessor, to advise on the spiritual or moral aspect of his decisions. The general, by constitutional direction, lives in Rome and does not habitually perambulate the Society.

The Society is divided into national or regional provinces administered by a provincial, assisted by four consultors appointed by the general, and by a spiritual adviser. The provincial appoints the lesser officials of his province and visits every house yearly, besides receiving each year a full report of its spiritual and temporal state. He in turn sends yearly a full report to the general. Access to the general is permitted to all, and from bottom to top a twofold current of information passes, from the superiors concerning their subjects and from the subjects concerning their superiors.

---

aut crebro fiat: quoniam Præpositus Generalis adjutus communicatione quam cum universa Societate habet, et eorum opera qui cum ipso degent, hoc laboris et distractionis universæ Societati, quantum fieri poterit, adimet.

[1] The dispensing powers of the Stuart kings, especially those claimed by James II, who, it will be remembered, had for a time the Jesuit Privy Councillor, Fr. Petre, at his elbow, were somewhat similar, but used in an invidious manner.

There is no provincial congregation with administrative or directive powers, and no conventual chapter. The two provincial representatives to the general congregation, in addition to the provincial, are elected by all the professed, rectors of colleges, and procurators of the province.

The Society of Jesus is thus an advance upon the Dominican order in the direction of centralization and firm rule. There is no democratic or elective element whatever in it save for the very occasional choice of a general, when the electoral body, the general congregation, is chosen by a privileged group of professed and officials. The Society indeed is in intention and by constitution a *corps d'élite* in the hands of a single commander. It is at once the end of a process of logical development from the monastic rules and the end of a flight from the monastic conception of the religious life. It is indeed both in character and purpose a new creation. The monastic rule and its mediator, the abbot, existed solely for the spiritual advancement of the community. The monk is indeed the soldier of Christ, but his warfare is internal and unseen. The friars were in this as in other ways a 'mixed' body. On the level of the community the end was the sanctification of the individual, but on the level of the order they were directed towards learning, teaching, preaching, and writing. With the Jesuits the end of the order as an order is sought and achieved *in foro externo*, by external action, directed by a single head.

Whereas a monastic abbot is, so to say, a correlative term to his monks, existing for their sake, and for their service rather than for their exploitation, and while the general and provincials of the friars are officers of their order, existing to develop and apply the resources of the community, the officers of the Society of Jesus are the lieutenants, one had almost said the sergeants, of the general. Whereas an abbot of monks or a guardian of friars exists as a shepherd, or even, in St Francis's phrase, as a 'mother' of those in his charge, and will, in St. Benedict's words, be called to give an account of their souls as well as his own, the Jesuit of the Constitutions is like a soldier, expendable; he exists to carry out the designs of his general and can be used, as soldiers are, to be risked and, if need be, to be lost. The analogy of course must not be pressed too far. The general cannot risk the souls of his subjects. Even on the purely human level a commander must care for his troops and shed as little blood as may be. Moreover, a subordinate officer must have initiative as well as submission. Nevertheless, the military metaphor was chosen by St. Ignatius and enshrined both in the title of company and in the founding bull of Paul III, *Regimini militantis ecclesiae*. We know from the life and writings of Ignatius that he always treated his men as individuals, never as counters or canon fodder, and that his intuitive sympathy and love were always at their service, but we are now considering his order in its formal, constitutional aspect, and as such it must be regarded as the most carefully centralized and disciplined non-military body that has ever existed.

IX

THE EVOLUTION OF THE DOCTRINE OF OBEDIENCE

A REVIEW of the constitutional development of the religious order over more than a thousand years, from the twilight of the ancient civilization to the dawn of the modern world, must start many topics in the mind of both writer and reader. One such matter, the development of the doctrine of religious obedience, may be pursued for a few pages at the end of our brief sketch, as being itself directly mentioned in the documents we have been considering. It is a topic which has in fact seldom been treated historically in its various aspects. But before beginning a chronological progress, it may be well to set out the accepted doctrine of ascetic theology on the subject.

The aim of the Christian is to conform his will in all respects to the will of God. We pray daily that His will may be done, and Christ has told us that he who does the will of the Father shall enter into the kingdom of heaven and, more briefly, that if we love Christ we shall keep his commandments. In order to do the will of God we must know it, and a Christian's knowledge, in the course of his life, comes from three sources, all of which are ultimately reduced to one source, God Who is Truth, and Who enlightens all His children in the way best fitted to their faculties and capacities. The three sources are natural reason, instruction from others in whatever way received, and the direct inspiration of God, all of which are part of every Christian's life.

Our natural reason, left to itself, is fallible, limited in its information, and limited in its field of vision. Yet in the ultimate moment of decision, we must act according to what we see to be according to, or at least not contrary to, right reason. But granted the fact of God's revelation of His will for men in the Scriptures and in the teaching of Christ as mediated by the Church, the normal means of instruction is the teaching of uninformed Christians by those better informed, and above all by those commissioned by Christ to teach. This is no more than an extension of the natural principle, *cuique in sua arte credendum*, that it is the human duty of the ignorant to accept the teaching of the wise. But in matters both of faith and action all men have a single Master, God Himself, Who can teach His creatures either through others or by Himself, and in the ultimate resort God's teaching, when clearly seen, must be accepted above all else.

Yet a Christian is not a being of reason alone, nor is it true, as Socrates may have thought, that ignorance and wrong-doing are convertible terms. Our will is limited in its power and weak to a greater degree than is our reason. Just as the reason needs the assistance of both God and man to inform it and to perfect it, so the will needs both the grace of God and the influence and direction of man if it is to achieve right action. It is on this need for human help, by instruction and by command, in learning the truth and in acting rightly, that the ultimate sanction of religious obedience lies. In both realms, of knowledge and of action, the need for human assistance may become less the greater the proficiency of the subject, and in either God can Himself replace all intermediate agencies, though He does not ordinarily do so. But in the realm of the will, two further considerations enter the reckoning. It is Christian teaching that the first and most fatal of all sins was a sin of pride issuing in disobedience, and it is common experience that pride, the quasi-natural unwillingness to submit to control, is the basic spiritual fault. Translated into lower terms, the terms of daily action, it is clear that in any social enterprise the submission of private interest and initiative to that of the group, or to that of some sort of ordered and directed action, is essential. In other words, obedience, beyond and above other virtues, is a practical necessity and an ascetical benefit.

Obedience, therefore, is an integral part of the Christian life in its personal as well as in its social aspects, and *a fortiori* it must appear in the life of the religious, whose aim is Christian perfection. Because we are men, and live among men, a part of our obedience must be to men, who in various ways and degrees represent God in our lives. Yet no man, *qua* man, is wholly wise or wholly good; he is not therefore to be believed or obeyed in all conceivable circumstances. Hence the problems and predicaments that surround the teaching of the masters of the spiritual life when they treat of obedience.

Monasticism, as we have seen, began with the retirement of the individual into solitude, and for more than a century the typical figure, the author of some part of the wisdom of the desert, was the individual ascetic who, strong in the clarity of his vocation, tried and proved by years of experience, which under God had been his only master, had come to know, with all the saints, what is the height, the depth, the length and the breadth, and the love of Christ surpassing knowledge. Such a one was rarely allowed to live in absolute solitude, and when a group of disciples surrounded his cell, the science or art of ascetical and spiritual theology was born.

In such surroundings and conditions there was no question of a Rule, nor even of constant personal supervision and tuition, but rather of what would now be called frequent spiritual direction, of which the *Conferences* of Cassian are an example. The disciple was expected to yield obedience to the master, who was *ex hypothesi* both holy and experienced, and to the examples of the elders, that is, to common experience and successful practice. This was the simplest and least controversial form of obedience; it was, one might say, obedience in its pure form, for, granted the conditions, it was wholly rational on both the natural and the supernatural levels, as being the submission of the ignorant mind and the weak will to the instructions and commands of the wiser and more holy master. Even here, however, the familiar technique of ascetical training begins to appear, and we see famous masters imposing difficult, incomprehensible, or even ridiculous and impossible tasks upon their disciples in order to create and strengthen, or to test and prove, their obedience.

Almost at once, however, the cenobitic type of monastic life appeared and developed under Pachomius, and in the matter of obedience, as in all else, that great master anticipated the creations of later centuries. Once the common life had been established, with large numbers and varied occupations, organization and discipline became social as well as religious necessities. Pachomius stands at the fountain-head of monastic tradition in making obedience the essential monastic virtue; the abbot is to be regarded as holding the place of Christ, and in consequence the obedience of the monk is obedience to Christ and the will of the abbot is to be taken by the monk as his own will. This was a doctrine not readily accepted in practice by those used to the greater independence of the desert, and Pachomius drew up a penal code to maintain its observance. He was a strict, if humane, disciplinarian, as was indeed necessary if the large communities, made up chiefly of recruits from the illiterate peasant class, were to be kept in order and in healthy contentment. The monk took no vow of obedience, but when the tyro took the monastic habit it was understood that he knew and admitted his obligations.

The teaching of the saints of Egypt and the East was set down by Cassian, Palladius, and others with a clarity and an accuracy unsurpassed by any later spiritual writer, and they covered almost every topic of ascetic and mystical theology. In his *Conferences* Cassian repeats the teaching of the desert on the authority and example of the elders, and in his *Institutes* he emphasizes the necessity and the value of obedience to superiors regarded as the representatives of God. His writings helped to standardize both practice and doctrine in the monasteries around the Mediterranean. Nevertheless, neither there nor in the Celtic monachism was there a comprehensive Rule, as distinguished from a tariff of faults and penances and a liturgical directory. The monastery depended immediately and entirely upon the abbot. Recent scholarship has made it clear that all around the northern Mediterranean from Cuxa to Vivarium, as also inland in southern Gaul, there was a single monastic atmosphere in which the abbot was a monarch without checks or controls, and the same may be said of the Irish monasticism, which was soon to be exported to the Continent. It is also clear that the Rule *Obsculta* (i.e. the Rule of St. Benedict) is full of borrowings from and recollections of earlier monastic literature, and is very probably based in large part on an almost contemporary Rule of the Master. Nevertheless, for the purposes of our review the Rule of St. Benedict can be considered (as indeed it was by all who used it) as a self-contained and authoritative piece of legislation. For the early Middle Ages, the doctor of obedience was St. Benedict, as seen in his Rule. Every reader of that Rule receives the impression that the sovereign authority in the monastery is the abbot. Once elected, he is supreme. He can appoint, promote, command, punish, and dismiss his monks of his own initiative and power. He must ask advice, but he need not take it. He orders the daily life of the monastery in general and in particular. For his monks he takes the place of Christ, and must be so regarded.[1] He is in office for life, and is answerable to no disciplinary machinery save in the case, mentioned but hardly imagined, of utter unworthiness. As has been well remarked, the Rule is an abbot's Rule; it supposes an excellent abbot governing a very mediocre community, or in spiritual terms a perfect abbot instructing a mixed group of many beginners and a few proficient. Indeed the authority of the abbot is so immediate and so universal that the reader inevitably supposes that the Rule must have been written for a community of moderate size with an ever-present abbot. Regarded more closely, however, the monks are seen to be protected, so far as a rule can give protection, by several safeguards from the dangers of absolute government.

In the first place, the abbot must never act against the law of

[1] *Regula S. Benedicti*, II. 2, 'Christi enim agere vices in monasterio creditur.' Cf. ibid. LXIII. 13.

God or the Rule.[1] It has often been said (the *Regula Magistri* may disprove it) that this establishment of the Rule as the common norm of action for both abbot and community is original in St. Benedict. If so, it must rank as his greatest single achievement as legislator; by it he debars the abbot from changing the character of the institute and its obligations, and he gives to the abbot a common measure of obedience with his monks.

Secondly, the abbot must remember that though free from human control, all his acts will be examined by the Supreme Judge when this life is ended.[2] This warning is reiterated some seventeen times in the pages of the Rule; it is evidence, not to say striking evidence, that the writer was fully aware of the dangers inherent in the possession of power, which he nevertheless saw as an essential constituent of firm government.

Thirdly, the abbot of the Rule exists, *qua* abbot, solely for the service of his monks. His rank implies no prelacy outside the abbey, no private possession of property, and no immunity from the strictness of the monastic life. Nor is he permitted to use the obedience of his monks for any end save their own good and that of the community.

Within the ambit of the Rule, however, the abbot can use his powers freely. The writer of the Rule had a simple outlook on the Christian life, and he wrote in a chaotic age when only simple conceptions could be appreciated and endure. In consequence, he sees obedience in its simplest and most primitive form, the execution of an order or charge, the act of a virtuous and humble soul which is the direct opposite of the rebellious, uncontrolled mind which the monk renounced when he took the habit and which he is combating in the monastic life. St. Benedict would certainly not have excluded the more spiritual aspect of obedience, the reception of the abbot's spiritual teaching, but he did not, nor could he, envisage

[1] *Regula* III. 11. 'Abbas cum timore Dei et observatione regulae omnia faciat.'

[2] Abbot J. McCann, *The Rule of St Benedict* (London, 1952), p. 167, notes the seventeen cases, *Regula* II. 6 and elsewhere.

the complicated situation which could only arise when the Rule was being slighted by both abbot and monks, and when obedience would be demanded in its name for actions contrary or harmful to monastic perfection. Nor does he distinguish between the obedience of human respect and mere weakness or pliability and the strong, spiritual obedience of the adult soul. The chapter on the conduct of a monk who is commanded to do the impossible only underlines this, for the impossibility considered is physical, not spiritual. To seek in St. Benedict for a survey in theological terms of all the virtues would be to demand an anachronism. Nevertheless, it must be said that while the teaching of the Rule on obedience is justly regarded as a *locus classicus* of Christian asceticism which has served as a basis for all subsequent treatment of the topic, it can nevertheless be understood in a purely material, superficial sense, as if every abbot at every level of human action or deliberation were actually Christ, and not merely his representative under normal conditions. St. Benedict's teaching is not weak, and there have been innumerable monks in history endowed with Christian fortitude, but what is true may be misinterpreted, and monks have on occasion failed to attain spiritual manhood through a purely human conception of the Rule. The attitude towards obedience, rendered classic by the Rule and dominating monastic life throughout the Benedictine centuries, had its obvious excellences, both practical and spiritual. It had, however, certain disadvantages. By concentrating attention on the spiritual value of unreflecting obedience it encouraged a subjective, voluntarist attitude of mind which placed the value of the act of obedience before the value of individual effort to ascertain and accomplish the will of God in the corrupted currents of this life, or rather, to speak more accurately, which made obedience the one and only means of ascertaining God's will. The Rule takes no account of the psychological fact that to obey from subservience or indolence or lack of principle is a fault as common as disobedience. Though under ideal conditions, no doubt, the abbot would do no more than apply the Rule, which itself is an approved application of gospel teaching, yet in fact the duty and value of uncritical obedience was to be emphasized under conditions very remote from those of the original monastery of Monte Cassino.

In the event, the growth of social and economic demands upon the monasteries of Europe and the weakening of observance made of the Rule as lived and of the abbot or his deputy who applied it something very different in character from the monastery and first abbot of Monte Cassino. When the community became very large and wealthy, and the abbot a territorial magnate on the fringe of political life, the constant daily interpenetration of abbatial government, regular observance, and personal spiritual direction ceased. The void was filled, if at all, by liturgical elaboration and by detailed uses and customs. The direct and personal guidance and governance of the abbot was replaced by the impersonal impact of an exacting round of observance, the *districtio ordinis.* The early customs of Cluny and the statutes of Lanfranc for Canterbury show a regular, severe form of life, but the personal, paternal guidance of the abbot has gone. The threefold intertwining cord of Rule-abbot-example of revered elders has lost one of its strands.

One of the consequences of the reforms at the end of the eleventh century was the replacement of the abbot among his monks, with the obligation upon him of implementing the Rule, understood literally, in the daily life of the monastery. We can see the result in the lives of St. Bernard, St. Ailred, and other saintly Cistercian abbots, even though they were engaged in frequent journeys, lawful indeed but lengthened beyond all expectation, on visitation and in attendance at general chapter. Of this new phase of monastic life Bernard was by common consent both the representative figure and the accredited spokesman.

Bernard, both in his own person and as abbot of Clairvaux, was an apostle of monastic obedience. At the same time he was a Cistercian of the first phase of the order's development, and thus one of the early recruits to a venture that owed its being to an exodus, one had almost said a break-away, from an existing Benedictine abbey. Much has been written in recent years of the character and aim of the departure from Molesme, and it has been the fashion to regard Cîteaux as a new, alternative version of the monastic life rather than as a violent reform, and to look upon Molesme as following a lawful interpretation of the Rule rather than a depraved version of the monastic life. This is not the place for a discussion of this important topic, or of the authenticity of the statement in one version of the *Exordium Parvum* that the first fathers had left Molesme because they felt that they had taken vows that could not be kept there,[1] but there is no question that Bernard in many places implies that many of the contemporary monastic uses were in fact abuses set up against the evangelical counsels and the precepts of the Rule.

Bernard therefore was in a delicate position. He could no longer preach a total obedience to Rule-abbot-custom as a single composite authority. The Rule now stood as a separate and in some ways superior authority to the abbot, to be observed, according to the Cistercian battle-cry, *ad apicem litterae*, 'to the last dot', and the individual monk had the duty, under certain circumstances, of examining the abbot and the traditions of his house, and of departing if they were found wanting. This is a topic to which Bernard was often drawn by events in the monastic world and by the queries of correspondents. His set reply, which in its tone reflects the maturity of his later years, is contained in his treatise *De*

[1] Cf. text of *Exordium Parvum* in J. B. Van Damme, *Documenta*. 7, where the reading of the Laibach and Zürich MSS., representing a version of the *Exordium* earlier than the final official text, is as follows: 'Nam viri isti apud Molismum positi [i.e., those who founded Cîteaux] . . . videntes se ceterosque monachos hanc regulam sollempni professione servaturos promisisse, eamque minime custodisse, et ob hoc perjurii crimen incurisse, &c.' It has not, I think, been noticed by continental scholars that the apologia of Prior Richard of St. Mary's, York, the leader of the exodus to Fountains, is clearly influenced by the *Exordium* and *Carta Caritatis* in their primitive forms.

praecepto et dispensatione, addressed to the monks of St. Peter's abbey at Chartres. This deals formally with religious obedience and considers its extent, obligations, and character. Wholly traditional in form and spirit, it is the first exposition of the subject in an age which was beginning to examine all problems in set form, and it remained a *locus classicus* throughout the Middle Ages. For our purpose, that of tracing the development of the idea of religious obedience, it is the incidental clauses that are significant, and they have been italicized below.

Bernard enunciates the principle as follows:

Only that which I have promised can be demanded of me. The nature of the monastic profession defines the limit of obedience . . . he who has taken vows cannot be forced beyond his profession by the law of obedience, *nor can he be kept from realizing what he has vowed* . . . still less can he be compelled to act against it . . . Therefore the command or the prohibition of the superior must not go beyond the limits of the monk's profession. . . . he may not increase the obligation of my vows without my consent, *nor may he lessen it without clear necessity*.[1]

The italicized clauses are perhaps inserted to safeguard an important principle which for the moment he does not wish to emphasize. They are in any case theologically and spiritually valuable, though the writer does not develop them in what follows. He goes on to consider the more common topic of the merit of obedience in positive matters beyond the exact limits of obligation—'Perfect obedience knows no legal limit'[2]—and to stress the motive of obedience, that the superior stands in the place of God; he adds that it is God's will that the subject is following rather than the superior who mediates it, but obedience will regard all commands as being God's will unless they are certainly contrary to it.

[1] *Liber de praecepto et dispensatione* in *Opera*, ed. J. Mabillon (Paris, 1690), I. 504 (= Migne, *P.L.* CLXXXII., col. 867): 'Professus nec ultra obedientiae legem cogendus nec citra est inhibendus . . . quanto minus contra . . . vota mea nec augeat [praelatus] sine mea voluntate nec minuat sine certa necessitate.'

[2] Ibid. 505 (*Migne*, col. 568): 'Perfecta obedientia legem nescit.'

Towards the end of the treatise Bernard discusses the possibility of leaving one's monastery to pass to another. Here again he was on delicate ground, with the origins of Cîteaux and his own *Apologia* behind him, but he was never one to let past events influence his treatment of present problems, and he answers as if he had only a theoretical question to settle. No transference is lawful, he says, save to a notably more austere life, and there are many lawful interpretations of the Rule, benign as well as severe. Even the Cluniacs provide a tolerable interpretation, and anyone who has accepted their way of life would do well to stay where he is, if his monastery is an observant one with good constitutions. Nevertheless, if the monk feels a permanent conscientious scruple, let him depart to a house where the Rule is kept in its purity. In any case, let us all follow the counsel of the Apostle (Rom. xiv. 3). Let him who goes elsewhere not condemn him who stays, and let him who stays not condemn him who seeks a stricter life. Wise practical counsel, we may say, but is it spiritually helpful? Is there not a level of observance beneath which observance of the evangelical counsels is not possible? It is interesting to compare Bernard's pronouncements as an elder statesman with his enthusiastic congratulations to the monks of St. Mary's, York, who in 1132 went forth to found Fountains Abbey: 'You yourselves have realized the danger, for those who have professed the Rule, of halting one's advance short of its purity (*citra ejus puritatem*) . . . your action, so noteworthy, so salutary, rightly gives joy to the whole city of God.' And to their late abbot he writes: 'I will say with absolute confidence what is the bare truth, that it is wholly wrong to try to extinguish the spirit.' And in another letter to the abbot of St. Mary's he writes: 'You should make provision lest your sons, who fear to remain with you in a lukewarm condition (*in mediocritatem*), may faint by the way . . . You should, as the prophet says (Isaiah xxi. 14), run with bread to meet those who fear to remain short of the pure observance (*citra*) of their profession.'[1]

[1] Bernard, *Epistolae* (numeration of Mabillon-Migne) xciv. 'Tibi

The widespread movement of monastic reform had indeed brought into the full light of day a dilemma which a simpler age had not considered: what was to be done if the customs of a monastery were found incompatible with the observance of the Rule, and if then the abbot bids the monk abide by the daily domestic practice? St. Bernard, speaking here in agreement with current tradition, bids the monk follow his carefully formed conscience, even against common opinion, and he is a witness to the essential role of the monastery and of the abbot as existing primarily for the profit of the soul of the individual monk, not for any external work or purpose.

With St. Francis of Assisi a totally new approach begins. There is a well-known story which illustrates part, at least, of his originality. He was present, we are told, one year at the annual assembly of all the brethren at the Porziuncola church in the plain beneath Assisi when a number of the learned clerks among the friars approached Cardinal Ugolino, who also was present, with the request that he should persuade Brother Francis to follow the counsel of the learned brethren in his preparation of a Rule for his order. They gave examples of the kind of thing they wanted from the Rules of St. Benedict and St. Augustine, and from the official Customs of the Cistercians. Ugolino duly passed all this on to St. Francis, who made no immediate reply, but, taking the cardinal by the hand, led him before the gathering of the friars and there spoke as follows:

My brethren, my brethren, the Lord called me by the way of simplicity and lowliness, and he showed me this way in all truth for myself and for those who will believe me and follow my way. And so I beg you not to talk about any Rule like that of St. Benedict or St.

vero, pater reverende, tam tuta certitudine quam nuda veritate ego dixerim, omnino non expedit spiritum velle exstinguere.' cccxiii. 5. 'Ego Bernardus si de bonis ad meliora vel de periculosis ad securiora voto et opere libere pertransissem, et illicita voluntate ad ea quae mutavi denuo recurrere praesumpsissem, non solum apostata verum etiam regno Dei non idoneus fieri pertimescerem.'

Augustine or St. Bernard, nor of any way of life save that which the Lord in His mercy showed me and gave me. And the Lord said to me that He would have me to be a new sort of idiot (*un novello pazzo*) in this world, and that He would lead us by no other way than this.[1]

The authority for this story is the *Mirror of Perfection*, which, critically speaking, is, as all students of Franciscan history know, a 'vast Serbonian bog, where armies whole have sunk'. Nevertheless, one does not need to be a Sabatier to feel that this saying (though not, perhaps, its setting) is surely historical—and even if it were not, it would still remain a genuine reflection of the spirit of St. Francis.

St. Francis was neither a legalist nor a reformer, but he must have known enough of the monasteries round Assisi to make him fear that his friars might suffer from acquaintance either with lax customs or rigid formalism. But there was another far deeper difference between his outlook and that expressed both in the Rule of St. Benedict and the Cistercian Customs. The Rule of St. Benedict is professedly drawn up with the early stages of the monastic life in prospect; the method throughout is to use the means of regulation and obedience to create the good habits and the pure intention that will lead the monk to do from love and of his free will what he learnt by the hard experience of patient obedience and endurance against the grain. Obedience, in other words, and the Rule are primarily means to an end.

Francis, on the other hand, in his own experience (and it is always his own experience that he wishes to share with others) had begun, so to say, at the other end. He had seen intuitively, or perhaps, to speak more correctly, mystically, in what lay the perfect imitation of Christ. He had seen it with the simplicity of direct vision, and the rest of his task lay in meeting the chances of life and dealing with means in the light of his immediate vision of the end. From this difference of outlook there issued naturally a difference in his attitude to obedience. St. Benedict, the experienced father and legislator, is con-

[1] *Speculum Perfectionis*, ed. P. Sabatier (British Society of Franciscan Studies XIII), i. 195–7.

cerned almost entirely with the monk's submission to his abbot and other superiors in all the daily life of the monastery till life ends. Francis, who, though an expert guide of souls, was not by temperament or gifts a legislator or an administrator, has a simpler, more spiritual approach. His teaching on obedience is therefore purely spiritual, and it is stamped with the authentic mark of its author; it is, in fact, unique in the whole of the great mass of spiritual teaching given by masters who have received the unconditional approval of the Church. It follows two very sharply defined and, in a sense, sharply dividing paths.

On the one hand, Francis asserts as strongly, if not indeed more strongly than ever before, the necessity and value of obedience in the religious life; in the daily life with the brethren at Rivo Torro and the Porziuncola he expected to receive willing, instantaneous, and unreflecting obedience even in things apparently impracticable or foolish, and his language is often remarkably similar to that used by St. Benedict. The superior is to be regarded as Christ, and the obedience is to be swift and willing.[1] Moreover, he himself, several years before his death, resigned the administrative control of the friars, and obtained from his vicars, Peter Cathanii and Elias, the appointment of a friar as his special guardian, whose commands he would follow in all the chances of daily life.[2] In the Testament he reasserts his desire to be a prisoner in the hands of another.[3] Finally, there is his well-known comparison of the truly obedient friar to a corpse, which allows itself to be shifted about without a murmur, and gives no sign of pain or pleasure or pride.[4]

[1] Thomas of Celano, *Vita Secunda* (ed. Quaracchi, 1925): 'Fratres carissimi, primo verbo praeceptum implete.' Cf. Ibid. 50: 'Si frater fratris prelati subditus non solum audiat vocem sed comprehendat voluntatem, statim ad obedientiam totum se debet colligere. Cf. *Regula S. Benedicti* V, 'Primus humilitatis est obedientia sine mora . . . ac si divinitus imperetur moram pati nescivit in faciendo.'

[2] Celano, *Vita Secunda*, 151.

[3] *Testamentum* in *Opuscula* (ed. Quaracchi, 1941), 80.

[4] Celano, *Vita Secunda*, 152.

On the other hand, Francis's conception of human authority is strikingly original. Those in office among his friars are not abbots or priors, but the servants (*ministri*), slaves (*servi*), and, most characteristically, the mothers (*matres*) of the brethren, and the conception throughout is not of patriarchal or official authority, but of maternal care. Furthermore, although the minister or guardian is conceived as taking the place of Christ, he is not, so to say, the repository or the oracle of the Rule. Francis, remembering his own direct vision of the life of Christ, and the direct vocation which he attributes also to all good friars, sets the ultimate loyalty there, and not precisely in the Rule. The 'way of life', the imitation of the life of Christ, is what the friar has chosen, and he cannot be called upon to surrender the immediate jewel of his soul. The brother is to obey his superior in all lawful things, even if he sees that another course of action would be to the greater apparent advantage of his soul, but if the superior commands something contrary to what his heart (*anima*) knows to be right, he is to refuse obedience and abide by the consequences. The significance of this should not be minimized. No doubt it had been accepted from the days of the desert monasticism that there were limits to the monk's obedience, that the subject was not bound to obey, was in fact bound not to obey, a sinful command, but the emphasis had always been laid on the benefits of humble obedience to mistaken commands and on the sacrifice of his will that a monk had made. Moreover, the examples given of sinful commands were academic rather than real—commands to commit adultery, murder, and the like. The originality of Francis lay in his recognition that every true Friar Minor had an indefeasible right to follow his call to the new way of imitating Christ which the Lord Himself had revealed to Francis. Thus in the *Regula Prima* Francis wrote:

If anyone of the ministers should give a command to any of the brethren against our way of life or against his soul's good [perhaps the meaning is rather 'against what he knows to be right, against his conscience'] the brother is not bound to obey him; since that is no obedience, in which a fault or sin is committed.[1]

It is quite clear that Francis has in mind here not a command to do something universally esteemed evil, but one that would go against what a truly spiritual brother would know to be against Christian perfection for him in his friar's life. In the *Regula Secunda* the passage is modified slightly as follows:

The ministers shall direct their brethren . . . not commanding them anything that is against their conscience and against our rule. The brethren . . . shall obey their ministers in all things that . . . are not contrary to their consciences and our rule.[2]

In the *Admonitiones* a slightly different turn is given:

If any superior commands anything that is against the conscience of his subject, the latter must not depart from him, even though he obey him not.[3]

So important did the principle appear to Francis that it is enunciated in general terms in the letter addressed to all Christians.[4]

Each of these two aspects or poles of Francis's teaching has met with serious criticism. His assertion of the indefeasible right on the part of the individual to spiritual freedom has obvious dangers, which he himself recognized, and it could

[1] *Regula Prima*, par. v, in *Opuscula*, 30: 'Si quis autem ministrorum alicui fratrum aliquid contra vitam nostram praeceperit vel contra animam suam, frater non teneatur ei obedire; quia illa obedientia non est, in qua delictum vel peccatum committitur.'

[2] Ibid., 71–72. 'Ministri moneant fratres suos . . . non praecipientes eis aliquid, quod sit contra animam suam et regulam nostram. Fratres vero . . . obediant suis ministris in omnibus quae . . . non sunt contraria animae et regulae nostrae.' Here again the translation of *anima* presents a difficulty.

[3] *Admonitiones*, in *Opuscula*, par. iii, p. 7. 'Si vero praelatus praecipiat aliquid subdito contra animam suam, licet ei non obediat, tamen ipsum non dimittat.' The last clause is usually translated as in the text. Possibly, however, the meaning is 'Although the brother does not obey him, he is not to dismiss that brother.'

[4] *Opuscula* 92. 'Nullus homo teneatur ex obedientia alicui in eo, ubi committitur peccatum vel delictum.'

not be expected to make any great appeal to the canonist or to the administrative and authoritarian mind. We can see from the documents that pressure was swiftly brought to bear on Francis, and that he modified his language in the revised rule. Within a century of his death the history of the *zelanti*, the Spirituals, and the Fraticelli showed, in various regrettable or tragic happenings, that it was a freedom that could only be bought dear. Subsequent spiritual writers have made little attempt to develop St. Francis's doctrine in this direction. It remains, however, authentically his, and as such worthy of careful regard. So far from being, as is sometimes suggested, a revolt of private judgement against tradition, it is in all essentials the teaching adumbrated by St. Bernard and St. Thomas Aquinas.

On the other hand, those who have wished to see in St. Francis one of the first leaders of the religion of the Spirit have been shocked by his desire to submit himself to a lowly brother, and still more by his simile of the corpse. Both F. C. Burkitt and Sabatier saw in this a painful deterioration of spirit in a sick and disillusioned man.[1] It may be permissible to suggest that both groups of critics have failed to rise to the height of their subject. Only a saint can experience and dare to express the two apparently contradictory truths that merge on the highest level: that he who loses his life shall gain it, and that only the man who has lost all personal and private aims is completely master of his soul, clear in his vision of the truth, and unbreakable of will.

The teaching on obedience of the Friars Preachers is wholly traditional. They differed greatly in spirit from the first Friars Minor, in that the latter were primarily following a way of life, the imitation of Christ, which they wished to share with all who would hear their good tidings, whereas the former

[1] P. Sabatier, *Vie de S. Francois* (ed. 1931), 354–5. 'Ce furent les instants de défaillance où l'inspiration se taisait . . . Ce soupir vers l'obéissance cadavérique témoigne de quels ravages son âme avait été désolée . . . Il est, du reste, absolument isolée.'

were clerics trained mentally and spiritually for a definite work, that of preaching the faith in all its fulness. The Preachers were nevertheless a novelty, not only by reason of their novel constitution, but because they were the first religious order to exist for the accomplishment of an external work in the Church. This necessarily gave to the superiors of the order a new function. They did not exist, as did a monastic abbot, purely for the purpose of teaching their subjects the way of spiritual perfection; they had equally the duty of deploying them in the best way possible for the purposes of their institute.

The early history of the Friars Preachers is in many ways a direct contrast to that of the Minors. From the beginning Dominic was conscious of the end to which his institute was directed, that of preaching the truths of the faith to ignorant Catholics and heretics, and his originality lay in the careful provision of external means to attain that end. Moreover, whatever his personal characteristics may have been, his early companions were trained theologians and lawyers, and the Dominican constitutions, as we have seen, are remarkable for their careful and complicated legislation. In spirituality, Dominic was content to draw upon the monastic and canonical past; in the next generation, a series of great academic masters, culminating in St. Thomas, set out the Christian and religious virtues in scholastic language. Consequently, the Dominican expression of the spiritual life has always taken a theological form.

At the same time, the institute of the Friars Preachers, by its very existence and wide success, profoundly changed the appearance of the traditional religious life. The earlier monastic and canonical orders, with unimportant exceptions, had carried on the primitive tradition of a self-contained community, existing primarily for the sanctification of its members, to which end all activities and all obedience could ultimately be directed. The abbot or prior was in truth as well as in name the father of his family. The early rule of Francis simplified rather than extended this personal, individual relationship of subject to superior. His original conception would seem to have been one of groups of friars under a minister or guardian, indeed, but going forth, of their own initiative, to find work or to preach penance. Even the choice of going out beyond the bounds of Christendom to preach to the unbeliever was at first left wholly to the individual brother. Consequently, while domestic obedience was detailed and absolute, what may be called external control scarcely existed, while the choice of work and its place and scope and, still more significantly, the adaptation of all activities to the friar's way of life, the imitation of Christ, was left to the conscience and spiritual judgement of the individual. Hence, as we have seen, the originality of Francis.

With the Friars Preachers, on the other hand, organization and direction were everything, and religious obedience was manifested primarily in the submission of the friar to the prior-conventual or prior-provincial in his occupations, studies, movements, and the whole external ordering of his life as one of a great and widespread body. The zeal and virtues of the early generations and their rapid expansion and rise to celebrity may have helped to conceal from others and from themselves that a new and influential force had appeared in Christendom, and that the traditional doctrine of obedience was now applied to a new and wide field. Moreover, the strongly elective and conciliar element present in the constitution of the Order of Preachers, and to a considerable degree also in the fully developed constitution of the other orders of friars, modified greatly the initiative of the general or any other individual superior. Finally, although each of the four orders developed a combative *esprit de corps*, and jealousy and rivalry embittered relations between them, the existence of four large bodies of similar character, and a sense of solidarity in their work and aims, may have helped to modify any tendency to exclusiveness on the part of one or other of the orders.

When St. Thomas, on his way through the various virtues, came to treat of obedience, he confined himself to traditional doctrine and made no attempt to expound or to meet the problems which St. Bernard and the Cistercians had posed. He based Christian obedience, which he regarded as a virtue of all the faithful, upon the natural law that inferior beings must be informed by those with higher knowledge, and that in any body of men it was of divine institution that some should command and others obey. On the moral and spiritual level, and thus particularly among religious, obedience (he says) is regarded as a necessary means of instruction and practice in the life of the evangelical counsels; it must not, however, be given to a command which goes against the will of God, or against the rule to which profession has been made.[1] St. Thomas would certainly have applied to the commands of superiors his teaching as to laws in general, that if they were not right and just they had no binding force, though he would have said also that the burden of proof lay always upon one who questioned the ethical and spiritual rightness of a command, and that in normal conditions both humility and common sense would demand acquiescence rather than criticism.

Much has been written in praise and in blame, both according to knowledge and also very often without understanding, of obedience as taught and practised by the Society of Jesus. Here we have nothing to do with the history of the Society, or with the effects over the centuries of the official pronouncements of the Constitutions. We are concerned, however, to examine how far the official presentation of the

[1] *Summa Theologica* IIa-IIae, Q. CIV, art. 5, ad 3. 'Dicendum quod religiosi obedientiam profitentur quantum ad regularem conversationem, secundum quam suis praelatis subduntur: et ideo quantum ad illa sola obedire tenentur quae possunt ad regularem conversationem pertinere: et haec est obedientia sufficiens ad salutem. Si autem etiam in allis obedire voluerint, hoc pertinebit ad cumulum perfectionis; dum tamen illa non sunt contra Deum, aut contra professionem regulae, quia talis obedientia esset illicita. Sic ergo potest triplex obedientia distingui: una sufficiens ad salutem, quae scilicet obedit in his quae obligatur; alia perfecta, quae obedit in omnibus licitis; alia indiscreta, quae etiam in illicitis obedit.'

virtue of obedience by St. Ignatius in the Constitutions is a development, or an alteration, of the traditional doctrine. It may be well to begin by putting before the reader the kernel of the Founder's teaching:

Let all make it their principal endeavour [*plurimum studeant*] to cultivate obedience and to excel in it, and that, not only in matters of obligation, but also in other things, even when no more is seen of the will of the Superior than a sign, without any express command. They must keep God, our Creator and our Lord, before their eyes, for it is on his account that obedience is rendered to a human being, and they must take care to act in a spirit of love and not with anxious fear, so that we may all with unshaken determination make every effort never to let slip an iota of perfection, so far as may be by divine grace, in accomplishing the absolute observance of all the Constitutions and the particular way of life [*ratio*] of our Institute. And let us with the greatest precision strain every nerve and all our powers towards exhibiting this virtue of obedience, first of all to the Supreme Pontiff, and then to the Superiors of our Institute, so that in all things to which obedience and charity may apply we may be instantly prompt when we hear its voice, just as if it were the voice of the Lord Christ, for it is for his sake [*ipsius loco*] and for his love and reverence that we give our obedience, leaving everything, even a letter which has been begun and not yet finished, devoting all our strength and resolve in the Lord to this end, that holy obedience both in execution and in the will and mind be always in every way perfect, and meeting with spiritual joy and perseverance everything that may be enjoined upon us, persuading ourselves that all is right, obliterating every contrary judgement and opinion with blind obedience, and this in all things ordered by a Superior in which it cannot certainly be known that some precise kind of sin enters. And let each one persuade himself that those who live under obedience must allow themselves to be carried along and governed by divine providence by means of their superiors, just as if they were a corpse,[1] which allows itself to be borne

[1] *Constitutiones Soc. Jesu* III. Pars vi, cap. 1, pp. 175–6. 'Omnia justa esse nobis persuadendo; omnem sententiam ac judicium nostrum contrarium caeca quadam obedientia abnegando, et id quidem in omnibus, quae a Superior disponuntur, ubi definiri non possit aliquod peccati genus intercedere. Et sibi quisque persuadeat, quod qui sub obedientia vivunt, se ferri ac regi a divina prudentia per Superiores suos sinere debeat, perinde ac si cadaver essent, &c.'

in any direction and handled in any way, or like a staff, which serves the one who carries it in his hand wherever and for whatever purpose he may wish to use it. Obeying thus, he must accomplish with joy of spirit everything for which the Superior wishes to use him for the benefit of the whole religious body, holding it for certain that in this way, rather than in any other thing that he might give, following his own will with a different plan, he will respond to the will of God.[1]

This eloquent and striking passage of the Constitutions, the outcome of years of experience and much deliberation, is nevertheless written *currente calamo*, as if it were an unpremeditated and spontaneous composition. The words and clauses jostle one another like the stones of an avalanche or the currents of a torrent, and the reader has to follow the impetuous writer for more than two hundred words in the printed Latin text before he arrives at a period.

This long paragraph is glossed as follows by an official Declaration:

Obedience is given, as to the act, when what is commanded is accomplished; as to the will, when he who obeys wishes that which he who commands wishes; as to the intellect, when he judges as does he who commands, and when he thinks that what is ordered is well ordered. And that obedience is imperfect when, save for the execution, there is not this agreement of will and judgement between him who commands and him who obeys.[2]

Several considerations impose themselves. The first is that much of the teaching, and still more of its expression, is traditional. St. Ignatius, as is known, read many of the ancient and more modern Rules when planning his Constitutions, and in addition to the classical doctrine that obedience given to a Superior is in truth given to God, which was expressed with lapidary brevity in the Rule of St. Benedict, the clauses insisting on instant obedience, with all other work interrupted, is almost certainly directly inspired by the same Rule.[3] Similarly

[1] *Constitutiones Soc. Jesu* III. Pars vi, cap. 1, pp. 175–6.

[2] Ibid. 177.

[3] *Regula S. Benedicti*, V. 'Ergo hi tales relinquentes statim quae sua sunt et voluntatem propriam deserentes, mox exoccupatis manibus, et

the well-know simile of the corpse was without a doubt taken from St Francis.[1] Yet at the same time, the teaching of St. Ignatius differs widely in spirit from that of the predecessors from whom he borrows his expressions. To begin with, he reverses their conception of the territory and scope of obedience; one might say, somewhat loosely, that he turns their teaching inside out. Whereas they are concerned with individual actions within the ambit of a life regulated by a rule, he is considering, or at least including, activities of all kinds carried out anywhere in Christendom or among the heathen. On the other hand, while they demand no more than a willing, unmurmuring action, he requires a positive suppression of critical thought and a positive effort of self-persuasion. Secondly, the immediate object of obedience for Ignatius is the maintenance of the way of life (*ratio*) and government of the Society, whereas the earlier writers direct the reader's attention immediately to the law of God and the teaching of Christ or (as with St. Francis) to the friar's way of life, the absolute imitation of Christ. In a word, the originality of the teaching of Ignatius consists in his transference to his institute and its manifold external works and organization of the claim to reverence and acceptance with which earlier spiritual writers had endowed their Rule and the precepts which implemented its execution. At the same time, Ignatius surrounded the individual designs and judgements of the superior with that aura of sanctity which earlier legislators had confined to his character as representative of Christ. Granted, the celebrated phrase *perinde ac cadaver* ('as indifferent as a corpse'), which has been the object of much severe and ill-informed criticism, is a literal borrowing from St. Francis, who himself, as we have seen, has been criticized and misunderstood. Nevertheless, there is here also a very real difference of context and scope. St. Francis is clearly alluding to the circumstances with which he was familiar from personal experience,

quod agebant imperfectum relinquentes, vicino obedientiae pede jubentis vocem factis sequuntur.'

[1] See above, p. 82 note 4.

when he was 'under obedience' to an unsympathetic and coarse-grained friar. The moves he was imagining were the purely physical and local movements, and the barbarous medical treatment such as he experienced in his last years of life. Throughout these he might still remain the captain of his soul. The corpse imagined by Ignatius, on the other hand, might be caught up in the toils of an intellectual or political manœuvre, in which he (or it) would of necessity act and speak as a rational and responsible being; to suffer and be silent would be impossible. Furthermore, Ignatius demanded the absolute submission of the mind, and the active silencing or blinding of personal, individual judgement. But it is one thing to silence argument and objection within oneself when an apparently futile or ill-conceived action is commanded—'theirs not to reason why'—and another to act blindly or against clear evidence in matters where personal and rational action is *ex hypothesi* required by the circumstances, such as the implementation of a policy or the maintenance of a theological standpoint on questions where the faith is not at stake, or in an ethical case of conscience where there are strong arguments on either part as to the morality of an act. Finally, whereas earlier writers had excluded from the scope of obedience not only commands openly sinful or directly against the Rule (and therefore *a fortiori* against the evangelical counsels), but even (as in the case of St. Francis) those that were against the individual's inmost personal convictions, Ignatius set the burden of an exigent proof firmly upon the subject, who must be able to prove (*definiri*) that a recognizable species of sin (*aliquod genus peccati*) is involved.

The official declaration rounds off the statement of Ignatius. The subject must not only renounce (*abnegando*) his own judgement and act blindly (*quadam caeca obedientia*), having persuaded himself (actively, that is, not merely by a simple recognition of the fact) that all is well, but he must agree with the one who commands him in will and in intellect, and judge what he commands to be good.

To understand this attitude we must bear in mind the

'voluntarist' climate of the age, which was in part the distant consequence of Scotist theology and Ockhamist doctrine, which had led to the abandonment of metaphysical certainty and of all confidence in the ability of the reason to attain to absolute or transcendental truth in moral as well as in intellectual questions. This had coloured all thought for two centuries, and had made of authority the sole support of faith, and during the latter part of this period it had become common to transfer to the ruler, set in his place by God, the sole right of judging, pronouncing, and commanding. Stephen Gardiner's tract *De vera obedientia*, and the arguments used by Thomas Cromwell against More and Fisher, and by Henry VIII against Robert Aske, passed without criticism in a society which saw in the obedience of the body politic to a single ruler the sole acceptable recipe for success, for power, and even for national survival. In every degree of life, and every act of the king and his ministers, the subject was asked to see obedience as a religious as well as a civic virtue. It was not accidental that Ignatius, who framed his order with a certain basic resemblance to that of the Order of Preachers, should have disinfected his Constitutions from all trace of democracy and even of oligarchic or conciliar elements. The individual was left without any share in government or legislation, and he even lacked the right of giving formal consent to what was enacted.

Ignatius, indeed, went further still, and encouraged and invited his sons to give him and his lieutenants their complete and absolute confidence. The Constitutions continue:

All are also earnestly exhorted to show great reverence, particularly in their mind and soul, to their superiors. They must regard Jesus Christ present in them and must reverence them in all sincerity as fathers and love them in Him. They should in all matters act so fully with a spirit of love (*charitatis*) as to hide from them nothing of their inward or outward actions or dispositions; nay rather they should wish that their superiors should know all, that they may the better direct them in the way of salvation and perfection. And for this reason all, both Professed and Coadjutors, must be ready once a year (and in addition as often as the Superior thinks fit) to manifest their consciences to him in confession, or in secret or in some other way, for such a manifestation is of great utility. They must be ready also to make a general confession, dating from their last general confession, to him whom the Superior shall appoint to act in his place.[1]

Here, at the beginning of the modern age, Ignatius returns to the primitive conception of early monasticism, that the abbot is in every way the spiritual father who knows every intimate detail of the inner and outer life of his sons. In that early age, the purpose of such a knowledge was simply and solely to enable the abbot to lead the monk along the way of perfection.[2] Ignatius had an external end in view as well as the internal, and in his hands, as we know, this intimate link was a means of great spiritual benefit to his first companions and to the early fathers of the Society. Such an intimate knowledge presupposed a small society united in its ideals and able and resolved to maintain the spiritual purity of its direction. How far such an intimacy was possible or spiritually profitable in a vast order engaged in active works is a question far beyond the scope of this book.

[1] *Constitutiones Soc. Jesu.* III. 177. This practice of 'manifestation of conscience' was copied by other orders and had undesirable consequences. It was therefore forbidden in the *Codex Juris Canonici* (1918) canon 530, as an imposed obligation, though permitted, and indeed encouraged, as a spontaneous act of confidence.

[2] *Regula* VII. 44. 'Quintus humilitatis gradus est, si omnes cogitationes malas cordi suo advenientes vel mala a se absconse commissa per humilem confessionem abbatem non celaverit suum.' This passage, which is based upon Cassian, *Collationes* II. 10, is usually understood by commentators of a voluntary, non-sacramental revelation of faults. *Regula* XLVI. 5 seems to envisage a slightly different, and perhaps a more nearly sacramental, type of confession.

INDEX

Abb. = abbey, abbot. A subject providing a chapter heading (e.g., Cluny) is not indexed within that chapter. v.s. = see under